TAKING WORRY OUT OF THE CLASSROOM

MINDFULNESS AND WELLBEING ACTIVITIES FOR SCHOOLS

KATIE SCOTT

Worry Out Of The Classroom – Mindfulness And
Wellbeing Activities For Schools
ISBN: 978-1-8383199-0-8
First published in Great Britain
in 2021 through Amazon
self-publishing service

Produced by samanthahoughton.co.uk

DEDICATION

I dedicate this book to my daughters Amber and Ruby who inspire me and make me proud every day. Without them I would not have the courage or determination to complete the goals that I have achieved.

Thank you to my Mum who has helped and supported me while I have been building my business.

WHY MINDFULNESS IN THE CLASSROOM?

As a qualified teacher and someone who has worked with children for over 25 years, I have an understanding of how the education system works and how it is not working as well. We also know there is a rise in mental health issues in children, which is proof that children are suffering with anxiety for reasons such as peer/social media pressure, meeting school targets and for some, living with dysfunctional home lives.

I know from many years of working with children that many suffer with anxiety due to curriculum expectations. If a child does not meet the specific expectations, then they feel unworthy and develop low self-esteem particularly children with additional needs. Trying to keep up with other children is unnecessary and humiliating. What one child may be good at, others may not. We all have our own unique talents which should be explored and supported.

We also know that children who are under pressure or have low self-worth find it hard to concentrate therefore this has an impact on a child's learning and focus.

We are expected to conform and teach children to work hard in school, follow the curriculum and meet specific targets to enable the school to become outstanding; however from my experience, children are individual and unique in their own special way. This suggests that the current rigid, one-fits-all curriculum, is not effective for all as children are feeling anxious and worried about how they are achieving. Children are creative and imaginative and they have their own special talents that we must preserve and nurture, because they are our future generation.

We should be focusing on each individual child's creative ability along with learning Math's, English and Science. Some children may struggle with their education but have the most amazing talent in another area such as singing, playing an instrument or sport. Although schools do provide a range of activities for children, if a child has a passion on one particular subject this should then be a focal point, allowing the child to put their energy into what they love and really enjoy, developing their creativity.

It is time for the curriculum to change and put our children's mental health and well-being before education. Self-love, self-acceptance and teaching strategies to reduce stress should be top priority. Once we do this, children will thrive more effectively and be willing to learn in a positive way. Once we work on children's well-being, everything else will fall into place.

Children are the same as adults. They have feelings and emotions, anxieties and stresses, likes and dislikes. If children become emotionally distressed there is a reason for this, whether it be upset, anger or anxiety, they will display their emotions in different ways.

As teachers we do need to support children's emotional well-being as for some children, we are the only people in their lives that may believe in them and give them a chance to shine. We are positive role models for children to look up to. Without that positive role model, some children will have no hope of becoming the best version of themselves. They will continue to have low self-worth and struggle to believe they are capable of great things.

There is a desperate need for children to be taught skills to help with their emotional well-being. Many of these life-long tools are in this book, including; how to connect to yourself, ground yourself and reduce anxiety. How not to dwell on things, take things personally or over-analyze and how to focus the mind on things that make us feel good.

This book has been created to help teachers and parents with a range of mindfulness and self-esteem activities that support children's emotional well-being in the classroom or in their home life. With a range of fun and engaging activities, this book has been divided into sections to help guide and improve children's self-esteem, resilience, positive relationships, focus, determination, cognitive development and to help reduce their stress.

ABOUT THE AUTHOR

Katie has been working with young children for over 25 years and is a qualified primary teacher and EYFS specialist. She began working with children in 1995 with a passion to make a difference to children's lives. She spent many years working in a nursery school, focusing on children's development and how children learn.

Although education is important to Katie, her passion was to enhance children's self-esteem and nurture their well-being; modelling a positive role model and helping children believe in themselves.

In her early 30's she decided to train to be a teacher and bring her passion into the classroom. During the beginning of her teaching practice she began practicing yoga, meditation and mindfulness. This had a great positive impact on her well-being and changed her personal life for the better. She could not understand why children from a young age were not practicing these holistic approaches.

During her teacher training Katie found it difficult that many teachers focused on education alone and not on the children's well-being and nurturing their creativity. She did not agree, like many teachers don't, on how the curriculum was delivered. Due to government expectations, many teachers are under immense pressure and do not have the time to focus on children's well-being. However, it is time for change and children's emotional development should be top priority as this will enable children to learn more effectively.

Katie trained as a Hatha yoga/meditation teacher and children's mindfulness/yoga teacher, beginning to teach the children whilst on placement. Following her degree in 2016 she started her business 'Little Sunshine Mindfulness and Yoga'. After all her training she decided to leave the school classroom as a teacher and instead focus on teaching self-love and mindfulness.

Katie has now worked in over 50 schools in the North West. She facilitates teachers' CPD (Continuing Professional Development) sessions, to support staff well-being and teach strategies that can be used in the classroom. She does a selection of sessions: An 8 session self-esteem programme, yoga, meditation and mindfulness. Her aim is for meditation to be part of the curriculum and encourage children to practice on a daily basis. 'Little Sunshine' now has a website subscription providing mindfulness, self-esteem activities, a range of meditations and peer massage to support teacher's planning and time management.

Katie hopes that soon the curriculum will be reduced in order to spend more time focused on children's passion, creativity, imagination and how to have self-love and acceptance.

CONTENT

INTRODUCTION

As adults we often feel stressed and anxious. We live in a fast-paced society. Life throws us some difficulties and we must work our way through these challenging times and build our resilience.

We all have a monkey mind, the little voice in the head, (chitter chatter) which can often talk to us in a negative way - it is the same for children. We do not know what is going on in a child's mind unless they communicate and tell us. So even the child who is sat quietly continuing with their work in school may have many insecurities or anxieties that they are not displaying.

In school we are taught to sit quietly, get on with our work, concentrate and listen. If a child has many things going on at home or in school and we ask them to concentrate, just like an adult they will find this difficult, as their monkey mind continues to overthink or worry.

Children should be given time throughout their day to experience stillness and quiet time and to connect to themselves, just like an adult. We need to take care of ourselves and our own mental health. If children are given this time throughout the day they will begin to understand the benefits of meditation and mindfulness practices which they will then use automatically when needed. With a regular practice, teachers will also recognize how this has a positive impact on the children's well-being and the change in behaviour.

To improve children's cognitive development, concentration, focus, determination, self-esteem, resilience, positive relationships and to reduce anxiety and stress, we recommend 5 - 20 minute meditation each morning and a short mindfulness activity after lunch during the school day.

Children have a monkey mind just like adults, so by practicing relaxation before their learning, the children are encouraged to relax the body and mind; this in turn allows them to concentrate and learn much more effectively.

Most holistic therapies anchor our thoughts onto an object. For example, during yoga we focus our monkey mind on the breath. During meditation, we focus on either the breath, music, a guided voice or fixing our eyes on one point. During mindfulness we focus our monkey mind on our senses. These are all ways of taking our mind from one thought and anchoring it onto something else, creating a less stressed mind.

If children are provided with these life-long tools, to connect to themselves, this will then give them the ability to help themselves and their own emotional development, not only now, but throughout their lives.

This book provides a range of activities for teachers to use in the classroom, or parents to use at home including meditations, mindfulness, as well as creative emotion and self-esteem activities to improve children's health and well-being. With over 50 activities available, this is an easy to use book to help as a planning provision for PHSE, which not only helps the children but supports teachers with planning and time-management.

HOW TO USE THIS BOOK

This book is split into two sections:

EYFS/KS1/KS2 (4 - 11 years) and

KS3/KS4 (12 – 18 years)

The EYFS/KS1/KS2 section is split into 4 categories:

The KS3/KS4 section is split into 3 categories:

Please note that many of the activities are sensory, so ensure that the activities are suitable for SEN as some children are sensory avoidant.

SECTION ONE - PRIMARY

AREAS OF LEARNING

Each activity describes the suitable age range/key stage, benefits, area of learning and the resources needed to support PSHE planning.

The areas of learning support teacher's planning and help identify how each activity is beneficial to the children's development.

These areas include:

Developed awareness and concentration

Understanding strategies to help manage feelings

Recognising feelings

Sharing feelings

Communication and language

Literacy

Mathematics

Recognising what makes them unique

Recognising likes and dislikes

Exploring materials

Physical development

Fine motor skills

Positive relationships

Building self-esteem

Using imagination

Understanding the world

Developing creativity

MINDFULNESS ACTIVITIES

MINDFULNESS

Mindfulness is when we focus on what is happening in the present moment. Often our mind is on autopilot, focusing on the past or the future. We may be concentrating on something that has hurt us in the past or overthinking something that may not even happen in the future. Both thoughts are wasted energy as the past has already gone, there is nothing we can do about it, and the future has not yet happened. The more we try to control a situation the more we suffer. We do not know what is going to happen in the future so we must surrender to what is happening right now.

When we consciously focus on what is happening in the moment, we are aware of our senses. For example, if we focus on our listening sense, our mind is concentrating on our listening rather than our monkey mind. When we focus on our sight, we are consciously aware of our surroundings which guides us into the present moment.

The more we practice this the more aware we become of our negative thoughts and we can bring our mind back to the present again, knowing that our thoughts are what create our anxiety and emotions.

Mindfulness activities for children help them to focus their mind on their senses, reducing their anxiety and stress.

Snow globe activity

Whilst shaking a snow globe, ask the children to have a look at how the sprinkles move around and then fall to the bottom. Explain that this can represent the mind. Sometimes when we have lots of things to think about there are lots of thoughts moving around in our head, just like when we shake the snow globe. When we stop shaking the snow globe the sprinkles fall to the bottom and the globe is clear. Our mind is clear just like this when we focus on our breathing or senses.

This is a useful visual to use in most mindfulness activities to demonstrate how sometimes when we are overthinking, our mind may seem to be chaotic. However, once we concentrate on the breath, the mind becomes much calmer and clearer.

Benefits:

The snow globe helps children visualise how our monkey mind may feel when we have lots of thoughts going through our head. It also demonstrates how when we stop and focus on our breath or senses, the mind becomes much calmer. We have different learning styles so using the snow globe is valuable for our visual learners.

Areas of learning:

Understanding strategies to help manage feelings

Recognising feelings

Resources:

- Snow globe

Suitable For:

EY KS1, KS2, SEN

Tense and release

Ask the children to lie down, with their palms facing upwards, feet slightly apart and eyes closed.

Ask the children to:

Squeeze their toes, squeeze, squeeze, squeeze, and release.

Squeeze their legs, squeeze, squeeze, squeeze, and release.

Squeeze their stomach, squeeze, squeeze, squeeze, and release.

Squeeze their shoulders, squeeze, squeeze, squeeze, and release.

Squeeze their arms, squeeze, squeeze, squeeze, and release.

Squeeze their hands, squeeze, squeeze, squeeze, and release.

Squeeze their fingers, squeeze, squeeze, squeeze, and release.

Squeeze their face, squeeze, squeeze, squeeze, and release.

Squeeze their whole body, squeeze, squeeze, squeeze, and release.

Take three deep breaths in and out through the nose and relax.

Benefits:

This activity was created to relax the body and mind, to provide children with time during their day to release tension.

Areas of learning:

Developed awareness and concentration

Understanding strategies to help manage feelings

Physical development

EY, KS1, KS2, SEN

Cloud activity

Take the children outdoors and ask them to lie on the grass and look up at the clouds. Ask the children if they can they see any pictures or shapes. Encourage the children to talk about the clouds; for example, what do they think a cloud feels like? Ask the children if they can feel the wind and what sounds they can hear. Ask the children to close their eyes, listen carefully and focus on their breathing.

Benefits:

This activity allows the children to be in the present moment, focus on their senses and be creative using their imagination. This activity allows children to relax and focus on their surroundings.

Areas of learning:

Developed awareness and concentration

Communication and language

Using imagination

Understanding the world

Developing creativity

EY, KS1, KS2, SEN

What can you see?

Ask the children to sit for one minute using a timer. Tap a chime or singing bowl to tell the children when the activity has begun and when it ends. Ask the children to take one minute to have a good look around the room and focus on their sense of sight.

Ask them to look for things they have never noticed before. Tell them to look high and low and out of the window. Then ask the children to put their hands up and tell you what they have seen that they do not normally notice.

Explain to the children that although they are in the classroom environment most days of the week sometimes, we don't consciously focus on our sight because our mind is thinking of other things.

Benefits:

Asking the children to take time out of their day to stop and consciously focus on their sight helps them to become more aware and present in the moment. This activity develops children's awareness and concentration.

Areas of learning:

Developed awareness and concentration

Communication and language

Building self-esteem

Resources:

- Timer
- Chime or singing bowl

Suitable For:

EY, KS1, KS2, SEN

What can I feel?

Use a range of sensory items to stimulate the sense of touch such as: elastic bands, water beads, spaghetti, leaves, gloop, shaving foam, playdough and place the items into containers.

Choose one child to blindfold and give them an item. Ask the child to describe what the item feels like and what they think they are touching. Ask the other children to say whether the child has guessed correctly.

Benefits:

This activity encourages children to focus on their sense of touch. It stimulates the senses and develops children's focus, concentration, and awareness.

Areas of learning:

Developed awareness and concentration

Communication and language

Exploring materials

Fine motor skills

Positive relationships

Building self-esteem

Understanding the world

Resources:

- Bag
- A range of items that stimulate our sense of smell
- Blindfold

Suitable For:

EY, KS1, KS2, SEN

Water bead activity

Provide water beads in a container and ask the children to close their eyes and move their hands around the beads. This activity can be used to relax the children whilst playing calming music or ask the children to describe the water beads and how touching them makes them feel.

Benefits:

During this activity the children's senses are stimulated helping them to feel calm and relaxed. It develops children's focus, concentration and awareness.

Areas of learning:

Developed awareness and concentration

Understanding strategies to help manage feelings

Recognising feelings

Communication and language

Exploring materials

Fine motor skills

Building self-esteem

Using imagination

Resources:

- Water beads
- Container
- Water
- Calming music

Suitable For: EY, KS1, SEN

Elastic band activity

Cut a range of coloured elastic bands and put them in a container. The children can move their hands through the bands, pulling, lifting and squeezing them. This activity can be used to relax the children whilst playing calming music or ask the children to describe the elastic bands and how touching them makes them feel.

Benefits:

During this activity the children's senses are stimulated helping them to feel calm and relaxed. It develops children's focus, concentration and awareness.

Areas of learning:

Developed awareness and concentration

Understanding strategies to help manage feelings

Communication and language

Exploring materials

Fine motor skills

Building self-esteem

Using imagination

Resources:

- Coloured elastic bands
- Container
- Calming music

Suitable For: EY, KS1, SEN

Gloop activity

To make gloop mix the ratio one cup of cold water with two cups of cornflour. Use the hands to mix. This activity stimulates the sense of touch and helps relax the children. The children can describe how it feels or listen to calming music whilst playing with the gloop.

Benefits:

During this activity the children's senses are stimulated helping them to feel calm and relaxed. It develops children's focus, concentration and awareness.

Areas of learning:

Developed awareness and concentration

Understanding strategies to help manage feelings

Communication and language

Exploring materials

Fine motor skills

Building self-esteem

Using imagination

Developing creativity

Resources:

- Water
- Cornflour
- Calming music

Suitable For: EY, KS1, SEN

Shaving foam activity

Provide the children with a tray and spray some shaving foam onto the tray. The children can then use their hands to stimulate their sense of touch by moving their hands around the foam and making letters, shapes and pictures with their fingers. This can be used to make lessons more fun such as phonics, literacy, art or maths.

Benefits:

During this activity, the children's senses are stimulated helping them to feel calm and relaxed. It develops children's focus, concentration and awareness.

Areas of learning:

Developed awareness and concentration

Understanding strategies to help manage feelings

Communication and language

Literacy

Mathematics

Exploring materials

Fine motor skills

Building self-esteem

Using imagination

Developing creativity

Resources:

- Shaving foam
- Trays
- Calming music

Suitable For: EY, KS1, SEN

Memory game

Place a range of items onto a tray including small, large, different coloured items. Ask the children to memorise the items on the tray.

Ask them to look away while you take away one item and then they will guess which item is missing. To challenge the children you can take more than one item away, add more items or move the items around the tray.

Benefits:

This activity is a fun and engaging mindful activity as the children focus on their sense of sight. This develops children's focus, concentration and awareness.

Areas of learning:

Developed awareness and concentration

Communication and language

Fine motor skills

Positive relationships

Building self-esteem

Resources:

- A range of items
- Tray

Suitable For: EY, KS1, KS2, SEN

What can I smell?

Using a range of items to stimulate the sense of smell such as soap, toothpaste, flowers, leaves etc. Place the items into individual bags. Choose one child to blindfold and give them an item to smell. Ask the child what they think the smell might be. Ask the other children to say whether the child has guessed correctly.

Benefits:

This activity encourages children to focus on their sense of smell. It stimulates the senses and develops children's focus, concentration and awareness.

Areas of learning:

Developed awareness and concentration

Communication and language

Exploring materials

Fine motor skills

Positive relationships

Building self-esteem

Understanding the world

Using imagination

Resources:

- Bag
- A range of items that stimulate our sense of smell
- Blindfold

Suitable For: EY, KS1, KS2, SEN

What can I taste?

Using a range of items to stimulate the sense of taste such as jelly, custard, rice, spaghetti etc. Choose one child to blindfold and give them a taste. Ask the child what they think the food might be. Ask the other children to say whether the child has guessed correctly.

Benefits:

This activity encourages children to focus on their sense of taste. It stimulates the senses and develops children's focus, concentration and awareness. N.B. Remember to check for allergies!

Areas of learning:

Developed awareness and concentration

Communication and language

Recognising likes and dislikes

Exploring materials

Fine motor skills

Positive relationships

Building self-esteem

Understanding the world

Using imagination

Resources:

- Containers
- A range of foods that stimulate our sense of taste
- Blindfold
- Spoon

Suitable For: EY, KS1, KS2, SEN

Mindful eating

Give each child a raisin or a piece of popcorn. Ask the child to place the raisin or popcorn in the palm of their hand. In silence ask them to concentrate looking at their raisin/popcorn. Ask them to think about what colours, shapes, and patterns they can see. Take around one minute to have a good look at their raisin/popcorn.

Ask the children to smell their raisin/popcorn. Ask the children does their mouth water. Take around one minute to smell the raisin/popcorn.

Ask the children to put the raisin/popcorn into the mouth and move it around with their tongue without biting. Ask them to think about what it feels like.

Does it feel hard/soft/smooth/rough/sweet/sour/does it melt?

Ask the children to bite the raisin/popcorn and listen to the sound. What sound does it make?

Ask individual children to discuss their sensory experience with the rest of the class.

Benefits:

During this focused activity, the children are asked to concentrate on a range of senses. This sensory activity allows children to focus and develop sensory awareness.

Areas of learning:

Developed awareness and concentration

Communication and language

Recognising likes and dislikes

Exploring materials

Fine motor skills

Positive relationships

Building self-esteem

Using imagination

Resources:

- raisin or popcorn

Suitable For: EY, KS1, KS2, SEN

Stop and listen

Using a timer, tap a chime or singing bowl asking the children to sit and concentrate on their listening for one minute. Explain that after one minute you will ask them what they could hear. Depending on the age group you can give a specific number of things to listen for.

For example:

Year 1 ask them what they can hear.

Year 3 listen for 2 different sounds.

Year 6 listen for 5 different sounds.

Benefits:

This activity not only allows children to stop and concentrate, it also allows children time out of their busy day. By stopping and listening they are taking their monkey mind away from negative thoughts and focusing their attention on their sense of hearing. This is a great activity when beginning a lesson or to help manage behaviour when children need a break. This stimulates their sense of awareness, reduces anxiety, and improves cognitive development.

Areas of learning:

Developed awareness and concentration

Communication and language

Literacy

Mathematics

Exploring materials

Fine motor skills

Positive relationships

Building self-esteem

Using imagination

Resources:

- Chime or singing bowl

Suitable For: EY, KS1, KS2, SEN

Partner listening

Ask the children to sit with a partner. Give each partner either the number one or two. Number ones will be the listener, number twos will be the speaker. Explain to the children the speaker has one minute to talk to their partner whilst the listener is not allowed to talk but to consciously listen. After one minute I will ask the listener what the speaker has said.

Give the children examples of what to talk about such as what they did at the weekend, where they are going on holiday, talk about their pet, their best friend or family. After one minute the listener and speaker will swap.

Benefits:

This listening activity stimulates the sense of hearing. This develops children's awareness, self-confidence, speech, language and listening skills. It allows children time to express themselves and build their self-esteem. It encourages children to be independent, use their initiative and team building skills.

Areas of learning:

Developed awareness and concentration

Understanding strategies to help manage feelings

Recognising feelings

Sharing feelings

Communication and language

Recognise what makes them unique

Positive relationships

Building self-esteem

Understanding the world

Resources:

No resources

Suitable For: KS1, KS2, SEN

Count the magic word listening game

Choose a child to stand at the front of the class and choose a magic word. Give examples such as the name of their pet, football club or friend. The child will talk for one minute including using the magic word in their sentences. The other children in the class will use a tally to record how many times the person said the magic word. After one minute, ask the children how many times they thought they heard the magic word.

Benefits:

This fun, engaging and interactive listening game encourages self-confidence and team building. It develops communication, speech and language skills, awareness, concentration, and focus.

Areas of learning:

Developed awareness and concentration

Sharing feelings

Communication and language

Mathematics

Fine motor skills

Positive relationships

Building self-esteem

Understanding the world

Resources:

- Paper
- Pen

Suitable For: KS1, KS2

Clap game

Sit the children in a circle. Ask the children to focus on their listening. Start the clapping game by clapping and tapping in a rhythm. For example, clap the hands twice, tap the legs twice. The child next to them will copy the clap and so on around the circle. Choose different children to start the clap. For a challenge use claps, taps, touch the head and click the fingers.

Benefits:

This interactive listening game improves concentration, listening skills, awareness, self-confidence, team building, taking turns and memory.

Areas of learning:

Developed awareness and concentration

Communication and language

Physical development

Positive relationships

Building self-esteem

Using imagination

Developing creativity

Resources:

No resources

Suitable For: EY, KS1, KS2, SEN

Bubble and name game

Sit the children in a circle. Blow bubbles into the middle of the circle and shout out a child's name. The child whose name has been called out, pops the bubbles. The children can count how many bubbles are popped.

Benefits:

This is a mindful listening game developing the children's focus, concentration, turn taking, patience and self-esteem.

Areas of learning:

Developed awareness and concentration

Communication and language

Physical development

Positive relationships

Building self-esteem

Resources:

- Bubbles

Suitable For: EY, KS1, SEN

Listening blocks

Sit the children in a circle. Using blocks call out a child's individual name to come and place a block on the floor. Continue choosing individual children to place a block on top of the previous one. Count how many blocks are placed before they fall to the ground. See if you can beat that number on the next game. The children must mindfully listen for their name.

Benefits:

This is a mindful listening game developing the children's focus, concentration, turn taking, patience and self-esteem. It also encourages children to work with numbers, developing hand/eye co-ordination.

Areas of learning:

Developed awareness and concentration

Communication and language

Physical development

Positive relationships

Building self-esteem

Resources:

Blocks

Suitable For: EY, KS1, SEN

Sensory bag

Place a range of items into a bag or boxes. Choose one child to come to the front and wear a blindfold. Explain to the children that the child with the blindfold will put their hand into the bag and choose an item. They will then use their senses to explain how the item feels, what sound it makes, does it have a smell. Ask the child questions such as does it feel hard, soft, long, short, rough, smooth?

Encourage the child to use describing words. The blindfolded child will then have a guess at what the item might be. Explain to the children on the carpet that they must not shout out otherwise they will give the person the answer. When the blindfolded child guesses what it is then ask the children on the carpet if the child is correct.

Benefits:

This fun and interactive game develops children's imagination whilst stimulating the senses. It increases the child's focus, concentration, self-confidence and team building. It improves children's patience, turn taking and develops children's use of descriptive words.

Areas of learning:

Developed awareness and concentration

Sharing feelings

Communication and language

Exploring materials

Physical development

Positive relationships

Building self-esteem

Understanding the world

Using imagination

Resources:

- Bag
- Blindfold
- A range of items

Suitable For: EY, KS1, KS2, SEN

Heartbeat stillness

Ask the children to stand up. Using a timer ask them to jump for 1 minute. After 1 minute ask them to stand still and place their hand on their heart. Choose some children to explain how their body and heart feels.

Ask the children to take 10 slow deep breaths in and out through the nose. Again, choose children to explain how the heart and body feels now compared to before.

Explain to the children that when they are feeling anxious or worried their heart beats faster, however, this activity demonstrates the power of slow deep breathing and how it helps the body become much calmer and more relaxed.

Benefits:

This activity is a good way for children to gain an understanding of how the breath helps us to feel much calmer and relaxed. By focusing on the breath when our heart is beating fast, it enables us to relax ourselves and feel less anxious. When we focus on deep breathing we are quietening the monkey mind. This is due to our negative mindset impacting our emotions and then our bodies.

Areas of learning:

Developed awareness and concentration

Understanding strategies to help manage feelings

Recognising feelings

Sharing feelings

Communication and language

Mathematics

Physical development

Positive relationships

Building self-esteem

Resources:

No resources

Suitable For: KS1, KS2, SEN

Body language

Ask the children to stand barefoot in a large space. Ask them to close their eyes and take slow deep breaths in and out through the nose, taking their time to focus on different parts of the body. Rolling the shoulders up and down, moving the head slowly from side to side/up and down. Moving up and down onto the tiptoes, lifting the toes up and down, off and onto the floor. Lifting the arms and legs slowly up and down. Ask the children to open their eyes and slowly and mindfully walk around the room as slow as they can. Thinking about each step as they touch the floor with their heel and toes, thinking about the foot lifting off the ground and the other foot lowering.

Benefits:

This physical activity encourages children to slow down and become more mindful of their movement. The activity increases children's physical, spatial and body awareness, reducing anxiety. Grounding activities allow the children to connect to the Earth and focus their mind on their sense of touch which reduces stress.

Areas of learning:

Developed awareness and concentration

Understanding strategies to help manage feelings

Physical development

Fine motor skills

Positive relationships

Resources:

No resources

Suitable For: EY, KS1, KS2, SEN

Grounding activity

Place a range of materials onto the floor in a line such as artificial grass, water in a tray, pebbles, large sponge and bubble wrap. Ask the children to take turns walking barefoot through each material. The children can be blindfolded or without a blindfold. Encourage the children to describe what it feels like using their senses; for example soft, bumpy, smooth, or spikey.

Benefits:

This grounding, sensory activity develops children's balance, body awareness, self-confidence, cognitive development and reduces anxiety. Grounding allows children to focus their mind on their senses rather than on any negative thoughts.

Areas of learning:

Developed awareness and concentration

Communication and language

Recognising likes and dislikes

Exploring materials

Physical development

Positive relationships

Building self-esteem

Using imagination

Resources:

- A range of materials
- Blindfold

Suitable For: EY, KS1, KS2, SEN

Grass grounding

Walking barefoot on the grass, ask the children to create a circle. The children will all face the same way, holding their hands behind their back, as they slowly walk around with their eyes lowered towards the ground. The children will be encouraged to concentrate on their feet touching the ground as they take slow breaths in and out through the nose. Explain to the children this is a relaxation activity as they focus on their heels and toes touching the ground when they walk around.

After the children have slowly and mindfully walked around in a circle several times ask them to stop. Then explain that this time they will focus on one foot at a time. As they breathe in, the right foot will touch the ground and as they breathe out, the left foot will touch the ground, continue with this rhythm. With each step they will concentrate on their breath, keeping the eyes lowered and hands behind the back.

Benefits:

This grounding, walking meditation allows children to concentrate on their sense of touch. It is a walking meditation as the children quiet their mind to focus on the breath and movement collaboratively. This activity improves anxiety, balance, physical development, awareness, concentration and focus. This is a useful activity if children are feeling stressed in the classroom for example before any tests.

Areas of learning:

Developed awareness and concentration

Understanding strategies to help manage feelings

Recognising feelings

Physical development

Building self-esteem

Understanding the world

Resources:

No resources

Suitable For: EY, KS1, KS2, SEN

Shell activity

Each child will be given a shell. Ask the children to be silent during this activity until the end when they can share their experience with the class.

The children will place the shell in the palm of the hand. Explain to the children that when they first looked at their shell they probably thought it was one colour but now you want them to mindfully look at their shell and think about if there is more than one colour that they can see. Can they see more than two colours on their shell? Ask them to observe their shell.

Next, ask the children can they see any shapes or patterns on their shell, what is the texture of their shell? Is it rough or smooth? What is the outline shape of their shell? Keep reminding them to have a good look at their shell. Ask them to listen and smell their shell.

Ask them to use their imagination and think about where they think their shell has come from. Ask them to turn over the shell and see if it is the same on the other side. What colours, shapes, patterns and textures can they see and feel.

When the children have mindfully observed their shell, choose specific children to share their shell with the class, describing it in detail.

Benefits:

This mindful sensory activity allows children to concentrate on their senses, quietening the mind and reducing anxiety. The children focus on their observations using their imagination and creativity. By sharing their shell with the other children, they are building their self-esteem.

This develops cognitive development and concentration.

Areas of learning:

Developed awareness and concentration

Understanding strategies to help manage feelings

Sharing feelings

Communication and language

Recognising likes and dislikes

Exploring materials

Fine motor skills

Positive relationships

Building self-esteem

Understanding the world

Using imagination

Resources:

- Shells

Suitable For: EY,KS1, KS2, SEN

Nature walks

Go outdoors with the children for a mindful walk or teach outside asking the children to focus on their surroundings. Discuss with the children about the different sounds they can hear, what they see, smell and touch. Ask the children to focus on their slow deep breathing as they take in their environment.

Benefits:

Being outdoors quietens the mind and revitalises the body. Taking deep breaths enables the children to concentrate on the present moment helping develop lung capacity and reducing anxiety and stress.

Areas of learning:

Developed awareness and concentration

Understanding strategies to help manage feelings

Recognising feelings

Communication and language

Physical development

Positive relationships

Building self-esteem

Understanding the world

Using imagination

Resources:

No resources

Suitable For: EY, KS1, KS2, SEN

Mindful walking activity

Ask the children to write on a piece of paper some mindful questions such as:

1. 3 red items
2. 3 sounds
3. 2 smells
4. 2 rough items
5. 5 blue items
6. 3 smooth items

You can challenge the children according to age by including more items, sounds, smells etc. The children then go into the outdoor environment, answering each of the questions listed and writing down what they have found.

For example:

3 red items may be a bucket, flag and wheelbarrow

3 sounds may be an aeroplane, wind and birds

Following the activity the children can share their experience and findings with the rest of the class. The children can either work in pairs, groups or individually.

Benefits:

This interactive activity improves concentration, focus, imagination, creativity, sensory stimulation and mathematics. This builds self-confidence and improves relationships.

Areas of learning:

Developed awareness and concentration

Communication and language

Literacy

Mathematics

Exploring materials

Physical development

Positive relationships

Building self-esteem

Understanding the world

Using imagination

Resources:

- Paper
- Pen
- Outdoor area
- A range of items

Suitable For: KS1, KS2, SEN

Mindful moment

Give each child a small piece of paper with a time of day such as brushing your teeth, putting your shoes on, walking to school, eating your tea. Ask the children to be more aware of their senses each time they are completing the action written on their paper.

For example when brushing their teeth ask them to think about the touch of the brush moving around their mouth, the taste of the toothpaste, the toothpaste moving down the throat when they swallow, the bristles touching the gums, the touch of the toothbrush in the hand, the smell of the toothpaste.

This activity is to encourage children to be more aware and mindful in the present moment.

Benefits:

This encourages children to be aware and mindful during their day. When we are more mindful our mind is focused on the activity at hand and we are living in the present moment. This develops our awareness. The more we practice mindfulness the more aware we become of our negative thoughts arising and can bring our mind back to the present moment. This activity stimulates the senses, reduces anxiety and improves cognitive development.

Areas of learning:

Developed awareness and concentration
Understanding strategies to help manage feelings
Fine motor skills
Understanding the world

Resources:

- Paper
- Pens

Suitable For: KS1, KS2

Monkey mind activity

Placing the children into groups, provide each group with the word 'monkey mind' written in the middle of a spider diagram. Ask the children to write down their ideas of what a 'monkey mind' may be.

Ask the children to discuss their answers with the class.

Explain to the children that we all have a monkey mind which is the voice inside our head. Sometimes our monkey mind can say negative things which then affects our emotions.

Ask the children to write down all the negative words they may say to themselves such as 'I can't do this', 'Nobody likes me' or 'I am not good enough'.

Explain to the children that just because our thoughts may say negative things, it is not always the truth.

Ask the children to write down how to change their negative self-talk into a positive one by writing the opposite.

For example:

'I can't do this' – 'I can do this'

Benefits:

This activity provides children with an awareness of our negative self-talk. Once children are aware of this, they can gain an understanding that this is just a thought and not always true. This enables children to think about changing their thought patterns from negative to positive. It develops children's self-awareness, reduces stress, anxiety and improves self-esteem.

Areas of learning:

Developed awareness and concentration

Understanding strategies to help manage feelings

Recognising feelings

Sharing feelings

Communication and language

Literacy

Positive relationships

Building self-esteem

Resources:

- Paper
- Pencils
- White board

Suitable For: KS2

CREATIVE MINDFULNESS ACTIVITIES

CREATIVE MINDFULNESS

When children use their imagination and creativity, they can express their emotions, develop their fine motor skills and stimulate their senses. The creative activities in this book develop children's self-expression, self-confidence and positivity.

Squiggle

Ask one child to come to the front of the class and draw a squiggle on the board. Ask another child to come and complete the picture using their imagination. The children in the class can then guess what they think the drawing is.

Benefits:

This activity builds self-esteem, team building skills, self-confidence, imagination and creativity.

Areas of learning:

Developed awareness and concentration

Communication and language

Literacy

Fine motor skills

Positive relationships

Building self-esteem

Using imagination

Developing creativity

Resources:

- Board
- Pens

Suitable For: KS1, KS2, SEN

Pebble painting

Collect pebbles from the beach or buy from a garden centre. Discuss with the children a range of positive words and write them on the board such as live, laugh, love, be happy, peace, strong, brave, kindness, grow, learn. Ask the children to paint a pebble and write on a word of their choice including some creative patterns around the edge for example rainbows, stripes, hearts or stars.

Play some calming or uplifting music to create a positive ambience.

Benefits:

This therapeutic and fun activity develops children's imagination and creativity, whilst promoting positivity. This improves self-confidence, self-expression and reduces anxiety.

Areas of learning:

Developed awareness and concentration

Understanding strategies to help manage feelings

Recognising feelings

Sharing feelings

Literacy

Exploring materials

Fine motor skills

Building self-esteem

Understanding the world

Using imagination

Developing creativity

Resources:

- Pebbles
- Paint
- Paintbrushes
- Water
- Aprons
- Washable table cloth

Suitable For: EY, KS1, KS2, SEN

Swirl and colour

Ask the children to draw swirls with a dark coloured felt tip pen around their paper. Then, using a range of colours, colour in the swirls to create a colourful piece of art. Play some calming music to create a tranquil ambience in the classroom.

Benefits:

This activity allows children to be expressive using art as a form of creativity.

Areas of learning:

Developed awareness and concentration

Exploring materials

Fine motor skills

Using imagination

Developing creativity

Resources:

- Paper
- Coloured felt tips pens
- Music

Suitable for:

Nature art

Take the children into the outdoor area and using natural objects such as stones, twigs, leaves, and grass, create their picture. This could be a picture of a face, patterns and shapes, or anything of their choice.

Benefits:

This activity allows children to be creative using natural objects. It stimulates their senses and imagination. Allowing them to create in a natural environment.

Areas of learning:

Developed awareness and concentration

Exploring materials

Fine motor skills

Using imagination

Understanding the world

Developing creativity

Resources:

- Nature

Suitable for: EY, KS1, KS2, SEN

Create a breathing picture

Ask the children to create their breathing picture.

For example, if we draw a square, we would move our finger across as we breathe in. Then we would move our finger down as we breathe out. And continue in this way until the shape was complete.

If they draw an 'S' shape as they breathe in, they will move their finger up the 'S' as they breathe out, and then they would move their finger down.

The children can use any shapes or pictures as a guide to breathing in and out through their nose. Ask the children to then share with the class.

Benefits:

This activity is creative and fun, allowing children to focus on their breathing techniques and how to manage slow breathing in and out through their nose. It improves self-esteem, communication, and relaxation.

Areas of learning:

Developed awareness and concentration

Understanding strategies to help manage feelings

Communication and language

Literacy

Building self-esteem

Using imagination

Developing creativity

Resources:

- Paper
- pens

Suitable for: KS1, KS2, SEN

Gratitude jars

Provide each child with a plastic cup, some stickers and a ribbon. The children can decorate the cup with stickers and tie the ribbon around it. Discuss with the children and write examples on the board things we are grateful for not only in our life such as health, family and food but things throughout our day such as a parent smiling at us, our brother giving us a hug or a friend helping us.

The children can then write down 3 things they are grateful for and put it into the cup. The children can take these home and each night before bed write 3 things they have been grateful for that day.

Create a cup for the class for children to discuss and write what they have been grateful for that day before home time.

Benefits:

This creative activity allows children to express themselves and use their imagination whilst promoting gratitude. Gratitude increases happiness by 25%. By encouraging children to discuss and write down what they are grateful for creates a positive mindset. This reduces anxiety and improves self-esteem.

Areas of learning:

Developed awareness and concentration

Understanding strategies to help manage feelings

Recognising feelings

Sharing feelings

Communication and language

Literacy

Exploring materials

Fine motor skills

Positive relationships

Building self-esteem

Understanding the world

Using imagination

Developing creatvity

Resources:

- Plastic cups
- Stickers
- Ribbon
- Paper
- Pen
- Scissors

Suitable For: EY, KS1, KS2, SEN

Family cup

Provide each child with a plastic cup, some stickers and a ribbon. The children can decorate the cup with stickers and tie the ribbon around it.

Discuss with the children and write examples on the board things we do to help and care for each other. Ask the children to write down each member of their family and a thank you message for each person on a piece of paper.

For example, 'Thank you Mum for making my tea', 'Thank you Dad for helping me with my homework', 'Thank you brother for helping me tidy my room', 'Thank you sister for giving me a hug'.

The children can then take their cup home and ask all family members to write messages to say thank you to each other throughout their week. At the end of the week they can read all the messages out to the family.

Benefits:

This creative activity allows children to express themselves and use their imagination whilst promoting gratitude. Gratitude increases happiness by 25%. By encouraging children to discuss what they are grateful for encourages them to create a positive mindset. This reduces anxiety and improves self-esteem.

Areas of learning:

Developed awareness and concentration

Understanding strategies to help manage feelings

Recognising feelings

Sharing feelings

Communication and language

Literacy

Exploring materials

Fine motor skills

Positive relationships

Building self-esteem

Understanding the world

Using imagination

Developing creativity

Resources:

- Plastic cups
- Stickers
- Ribbon
- Paper
- Pen
- Scissors
- Whiteboard or IWB

Suitable For: EY, KS1, KS2, SEN

Lavender bags

Provide each child with a patterned or plain piece of square material, some ribbon and a cup of dried lavender.

Ask the children to smell the lavender and discuss the smell such as do they like/dislike the smell? What does it remind them of? Does it help them feel calmer?

The children pour the dry lavender into the middle of their material. They then bring together the corners of the material, hold and twist. This should now look like a small bag of lavender. Tie the ribbon around the twist, into a bow, to keep the bag secure.

Explain to the children that lavender has a calming smell. If the children put the bag in their bedroom, each time they walk into their room the smell will remind them to be relaxed. Also explain that lavender is effective for children who struggle with sleep therefore putting the lavender bag near to their pillow at bedtime can reduce anxiety and help them sleep better.

This can also be carried around as a reminder when feeling anxious as a comfort.

Benefits:

This engaging and creative activity provides children with a tool to help them feel relaxed and calm, reducing anxiety. It helps children when they struggle with sleep as they focus their mind on their sense of smell before bed.

Areas of learning:

Understanding strategies to help manage feelings

Recognising feelings

Communication and language

Exploring materials

Fine motor skills

Developing creativity

Resources:

- Square material
- Dry lavender
- Ribbon

Suitable For: KS1, KS2, SEN

Affirmation bracelets

Ask the children to write down a list of positive affirmations or words on a piece of paper such as 'I am strong', 'I am beautiful', 'Happiness', 'Peace'.

Discuss the list with the class and write examples on the board. Provide each child with a long piece of paper and some glue. Ask the children to decorate and create an affirmation bracelet writing down an affirmation or positive word of their choice.

When they have finished, glue the bracelet around the wrist. Choose some children to come up and share with the class. Explain each time they feel sad or unhappy their bracelet will remind them to feel better.

Benefits:

This fun and creative activity allows the children to express themselves and use their imagination. It promotes positivity and self–expression which reduces anxiety and stress.

Areas of learning:

Developed awareness and concentration

Understanding strategies to help manage feelings

Recognising feelings

Sharing feelings

Communication and language

Literacy

Exploring materials

Fine motor skills

Positive relationships

Building self-esteem

Developing creativity

Resources:

- Paper
- Coloured pens
- Glue
- Scissors
- Whiteboard or IWB

Suitable For: KS1, KS2, SEN

Mindful colouring

Using a mindful colouring book, photocopy some pictures and provide for each child with some coloured pencils. Ask the children to sit quietly while colouring. Play some calming music to create a relaxing ambience.

Benefits:

Mindful colouring allows children to relax, reduces anxiety and improves concentration. This is a therapeutic and calming activity that increases awareness and focus.

Areas of learning:

Developed awareness and concentration

Understanding strategies to help manage feelings

Exploring materials

Fine motor skills

Developing creativity

Resources:

- Mindful colouring book
- Photocopier
- Paper
- Coloured pencils
- Calming music

Suitable For: EY, KS1, KS2, SEN

Alphabet I am…

Ask the children to write down at the top of their paper 'I am…' Ask them to write the alphabet down the side of their paper. Discuss and write down on the board words we can use in a positive way, in alphabetical order, to finish the sentence 'I am…'

For example; 'I am Amazing', 'I am Beautiful', 'I am Caring' and so on. At the end of the session go around the class and ask each child to share a letter.

Benefits:

This is a fun activity that boosts self-esteem and confidence. By asking the children to focus on all their good qualities about themselves they are creating positivity. This develops speech, language and writing skills.

Areas of learning:

Understanding strategies to help manage feelings

Literacy

Communication and language

Fine motor skills

Building self-esteem

Using imagination

Developing creativity

Resources:

- Paper
- Pencil
- Board or IWB

Suitable For: KS1, KS2

Paper plate mandalas

Provide each child with a paper plate and coloured pencils or pens. Demonstrate on the board what a mandala looks like. Ask the children to create their own mandala using patterns, shapes and colours moving around the plate. You can either start from the outside and work your way in or start from the middle and work your way out.

A mandala is developed through self-expression and creative art therefore it is the child's own personal design. Play some calming music to help the children feel relaxed.

Benefits:

Mandalas are created through self-expression to express how you feel therefore it is the child's own personal design. By allowing children time to express themselves through art, they develop their creativity and focus, reducing stress and anxiety.

Areas of learning:

Developed awareness and concentration

Understanding strategies to help manage feelings

Mathematics

Exploring materials

Fine motor skills

Using imagination

Developing creativity

Resources:

- Paper
- Coloured pencils or pens
- Board or IWB

- Examples of mandalas for children to look at

Suitable For: EY, KS1, KS2, SEN

Playdough and pom poms

Provide the children with some playdough. Ask the children to roll the playdough into a long snake. Make a swirl with the playdough onto the table. Place a pom pom at the edge of the swirl and slowly blow the pom pom around the swirl until it meets the middle. The children can have a competition playing in pairs who can blow their pom pom into the middle of the swirl the quickest.

Benefits:

This mindful activity allows the children to focus their concentration on the breath. The playdough rolling is a calming and therapeutic activity developing physical development and concentration.

Areas of learning:

Developed awareness and concentration

Exploring materials

Fine motor skills

Positive relationships

Building self-esteem

Developing creativity

Resources:

- Playdough
- Pom poms

Suitable For: EY, KS1, KS2, SEN

Swirl drawing

Provide the children with a piece of paper and a pencil. Ask the children to place the point of their pencil in the middle of the paper and draw a swirl, moving around and around from the middle until it reaches the outside of the paper.

Ask the children to slowly use their finger to mindfully move in between the lines from the middle to the outside. Then ask the children to use a coloured pencil or pen to slowly draw, from the middle to the outside, in between the lines, without touching the sides.

Benefits:

This is a calming, therapeutic, mindful activity helping children to relax and focus their mind. It improves cognitive development, focus and concentration. By drawing slowly and not touching the sides the children concentrate and take their time which increases patience and determination. This also supports hand and eye co-ordination.

Areas of learning:

Developed awareness and concentration

Literacy

Mathematics

Fine motor skills

Developing creativity

Resources:

- Paper
- Pencils
- Coloured pencils or pens

Suitable For: KS1, KS2, SEN

Playdough activity

Provide the children with some playdough. Ask them to roll the playdough in the palm of the hand, flatten the playdough, make a snake, make a ball, poke their finger into it, create a circle, a square and a triangle. Ask the children to smell the playdough and discuss what it smells and feels like. Then the children can make an item of their choice.

Benefits:

Playing with playdough is very therapeutic. By asking the children to make several different things with the playdough helps them concentrate on their sense of touch. This develops their physical development and stimulates their senses, reducing anxiety and stress.

Areas of learning:

Developed awareness and concentration

Understanding strategies to help manage feelings

Exploring materials

Fine motor skills

Using imagination

Developing creativity

Suitable For: EY, KS1, KS2, SEN

Peg activity

Provide the children with some wooden pegs, string, paper and coloured pencils. Cut the paper into triangles. Explain that they are making their own positive bunting.

The children can decorate each triangle with positive affirmations and drawings such as rainbows, sunshines, stars, or smiley faces to hang in their bedroom or around the classroom.

Ask the children to read their affirmations each morning.

Benefits:

This develops children's creativity and art. It promotes positivity and improves focus and concentration.

Areas of learning:

Developed awareness and concentration

Understanding strategies to help manage feelings

Literacy

Mathematics

Exploring materials

Fine motor skills

Using imagination

Developing creativity

Resources:

- Pegs
- String
- Paper
- Coloured pencils

Suitable For: EY, KS1, KS2, SEN

EMOTIONAL ACTIVITIES

EMOTIONS

Emotion activities help children to deal with feelings and look at different ways to overcome difficult situations, helping change a negative mindset into a positive one. They help children better understand how their behaviour effects an outcome and how to take responsibility.

Line of day

Drawing a line explain to the children that this represents your day. The beginning of the line is the beginning of the day and the end of the line is the end of the day.

Draw a smiley face at the beginning of the line explaining that when you woke up you felt happy and content. Move a quarter along the line and draw a picture of a sad face at breaktime. Explain as an example that someone had pushed you over on the playground so now you are feeling sad.

Now explain to the children that this was just a moment and we should not let one small incident affect our whole day.

Using the line as a visual, explain how something can affect our whole day but we can continue the day more positively if we let go of what happened at the time.

Continuing along the line draw a picture of smiley faces at lunchtime, home time and bedtime as the child has not let one small incident affect their whole day.

Explain that it is normal to feel these emotions when someone hurts us, however if we understand that it is just one moment in the day we can continue to feel positive again and not over think or dwell on the situation.

Benefits:

This activity demonstrates how we should not let one incident affect our whole day. This promotes positivity and resilience. Using the line as a visual to provide a better understanding of how to deal with emotions.

Areas of learning:

Understanding strategies to help manage feelings

Recognising feelings

Sharing feelings

Communication and language

Literacy

Building self-esteem

Understanding the world

Resources:

- Interactive whiteboard
- Pen

Suitable For: KS2

Expressive writing

Provide the children with a pen and paper and ask them to create a poem or a rap about being happy. The children may plan their writing by making a list of rhyming words. The start of the poetry, rap or writing might be 'When I am happy I.........' Play some calming music in the classroom to create a tranquil ambience.

Benefits:

This activity allows the children to express themselves using creative writing, providing the children with a focus, promoting positivity and self-esteem. When the writing is complete, ask the children to share with the class.

Areas of learning:

Developed awareness and concentration

Understanding strategies to help manage feelings

Recognising feelings

Sharing feelings

Communication and language

Literacy

Recognise what makes them unique

Fine motor skills

Building self-esteem

Using imagination

Developing creativity

Resources:

- Paper

- Pens
- Music

Suitable For: KS2, SEN

Match the emotions

Using two pieces of paper, per two children, draw a grid of six on each. On one paper, write an emotion in each grid such as happy, sad, angry, excited, confused or frustrated.

On the other paper, write a description of each emotion in each grid, then cut out each description.

Put the children into pairs and provide them with a grid with emotions and six descriptions for them to match.

When the children have completed the activity, ask them to share with the class, to see if they have matched the emotion to the description correctly.

Benefits:

This activity allows the children to recognise their emotions and understand how emotion makes them feel. It is a good opportunity for them to recognise that everyone has these emotions and will feel the same. The activity builds self-esteem, positive relationships, and communication.

Areas of learning:

Recognising feelings

Sharing feelings

Communication and language

Fine motor skills

Positive relationships

Building self-esteem

Resources:

- Paper

- Pens

Suitable for: KS2

Art

Ask the children to draw a picture in silence using some calming music, either using crayons, coloured pencils or paints. You may want to use other materials such as glitter, sequins, utensils. Move around the class and ask the children questions such as:

What have you drawn?

Why do you think you have drawn that?

What does this mean?

How does this picture make you feel?

Following the activity ask the children if they would like to share their picture.

Benefits:

Art is a form of expression and creativity. Allowing children to express themselves through art is a good way for them to share emotions and ideas. It reduces stress and anxiety, developing creativity and self-expression.

Areas of learning:

Developed awareness and concentration

Understanding strategies to help manage feelings

Recognising feelings

Sharing feelings

Communication and language

Recognise what makes them unique

Exploring materials

Fine motor skills

Building self-esteem

Using imagination

Developing creativity

Resources:

- Paper
- Crayons, pencils or paint
- Paint brushes
- Water

Suitable For: EY, KS1, KS2, SEN

Stress bucket

Discuss with the children about things that make them stressed or anxious. Using a bucket template demonstrate the things that have made you stressed for example being stuck in traffic.

Provide the children with a template and ask them to write or draw pictures of things that make them anxious and stressed inside the bucket.

Use your bucket template to demonstrate to the children that sometimes when our bucket of stress becomes full and overflows, this then affects our daily life for example making us feel anxious or have panic attacks.

Draw a tap in your bucket and discuss with the class ways they can help release some of that stress for example practicing meditation, being in nature, telling someone they trust, doing something they enjoy, mindful colouring, breathing techniques.

Ask the children to go back to their bucket, draw a tap and write down ways they can release some of their stress.

Share the children's ideas with the class.

Benefits:

This activity is providing a safe and secure space for children to discuss what situations make them feel anxious. Using the bucket as a visual they can see how once it fills up, it can then become a problem therefore demonstrating the importance of using strategies to help release some of their stress.

Areas of learning:

Understanding strategies to help manage feelings

Recognising feelings

Sharing feelings

Communication and language

Literacy

Fine motor skills

Positive relationships

Building self-esteem

Resources:

- Bucket template
- pencils

Suitable For: KS1, KS2, SEN

Draw emotions

Discuss with the children about different emotions that we might feel. Talk about anger and how this makes us feel inside our body.

Discuss with the children what ways we can help ourselves when we feel angry. This could be using a stop button (pressing an imaginary button on our hip and taking deep breaths) breathing techniques, counting to 10, having some time out, going for a walk in nature, listening to some calming music or doing some mindful colouring. Encourage the children to come up with their own ideas of how they can help themselves.

Using a body template ask the children to colour code different areas to show how it makes them feel in their body. For example, the child may colour red arms and legs as this part of the body feels hot. The face may be green which is colour coded as feeling tingly and the heart may be blue colour coded as feeling cold. There is no right or wrong answer for a child to complete this. It is used for the child to express themselves and may be an opportunity for a child to express their emotions and feelings.

Benefits:

This activity is providing a safe and secure space for children to express how they feel. It is offering the child an opportunity to gain more understanding and awareness of their emotions and how to deal with these feelings once they arise. This will allow children to control their feelings in a more effective way.

Areas of learning:

Developed awareness and concentration

Understanding strategies to help manage feelings

Recognising feelings

Sharing feelings

Communication and language

Literacy

Mathematics

Fine motor skills

Positive relationships

Building self-esteem

Resources:

- Body template
- Coloured pencils or pens

Suitable For: KS2

Anger – scenario

Discuss with the children and write on the board

- What makes us angry?
- How does it make us feel in the body? (e.g. sweaty palms, clenched teeth, shoulders raised, feeling emotional)

Ask two children to come to the front of the class. Ask child one to pretend to throw a pencil at child two. Ask child two how they would feel and how they would react.

Ask the children in the class to take one minute to discuss with their partner

- How would you feel if someone threw a pencil at you?
- How would you react?

Discuss with the class their answers and explain that we all feel frustrated at times and that some people are more sensitive than others.

Using the two children again, explain that if the child retaliates with aggression, throws something back, storms out of the class and gets into trouble with the teacher and parents, this behaviour will not make them feel good.

Use the examples of how it makes us feel when we are angry to demonstrate the negative impact that anger has on our body and emotions.

Discuss with the class how things could have been different in this case by using calming strategies to help them such as slow breathing, time out, meditation, walking in nature, listening to calming music. Explain that we all have a choice and it is about making the best choice that makes us feel good.

Benefits:

Through discussion the children can gain an understanding that we all feel frustrated at times. Providing strategies that children can use to help deal with their emotions will give them the opportunity to help themselves feel calmer in difficult situations. This highlights that we all have choices. This activity develops resilience, self-awareness, positive relationships and reduces anxiety.

Areas of learning:

Understanding strategies to help manage feelings

Recognising feelings

Sharing feelings

Communication and language

Positive relationships

Resources:

- Whiteboard or IWB

Suitable For: KS2

The road ahead – choices

Ask the children to fast forward to the age of 25. Ask them to draw a spider diagram, writing their name in the middle. Around the outside of their name ask them to write down how they see their life at this age for example having lots of friends, what job would they like, where they would like to live, where would they go on holiday, what hobbies they would have.

Discuss with the class what they have written.

Ask the children to think about how they will achieve these things, for example; working hard at school, being kind to people, focusing on their own individual goals. Explain that we can achieve anything through hard work and determination.

Benefits:

This activity improves children's focus, determination, and resilience, creating positivity and developing awareness of how our behaviour and choices create a positive outcome. The children can use their imagination and produce goal settings.

Areas of learning:

Sharing feelings

Communication and language

Literacy

Recognise what makes them unique

Recognising likes and dislikes

Positive relationships

Building self-esteem

Using imagination

Understanding the world

Developing creativity

Resources:

- Paper
- Pencils

Suitable For: KS2

Shake the bottle

Sit the children in a circle. Explain to the children that you have had a stressful morning. Each stressful occurrence that you discuss, shake the fizzy drink. For example; your children would not get ready for school, you could not find your shoes, you were late for work, your car would not start, you were stuck in traffic.

Explain that shaking the bottle of fizzy drink is a representation of feeling frustrated.

Now pass the bottle around the circle asking the children to tell one thing that made them frustrated that day. Once the bottle has moved around the circle ask one child what they think will happen if they opened the bottle.

Explain that this is how we feel sometimes when things keep going wrong and we feel like we are going to explode just like the fizzy drink. Discuss with the children ways to help them during these times for example practice some meditation, yoga, calming breathing, stop button, timeout, counting, listen to calming music, being more organised.

Benefits:

The children gain an understanding that we all have difficult and frustrating situations at times. This activity provides children with tools to help deal with negative emotions, improving resilience and reducing anxiety and stress.

Areas of learning:

Developed awareness and concentration

Understanding strategies to help manage feelings

Recognising feelings

Sharing feelings

Communication and language

Positive relationships

Building self-esteem

Resources:

- Bottle of fizzy drinks

Suitable For: KS1, KS2, SEN

Passing emotions/clouds

Discuss with the children, what emotions are, asking them to write down as many positive and negative emotions as they can. For example; happy, sad, excited, angry, confused. Talk about how each emotion makes them feel and when do we have these emotions.

Explain to the children that emotions are like clouds and they come and go. One cloud could represent a sad emotion which passes, one cloud could represent anger which passes. Explain that we all have different emotions and it is good to express how we feel, however, it is important to know that this is just a moment and this time will pass.

Benefits:

Children feel overwhelmed when they feel negative emotions therefore this activity reminds children that it is okay to feel these feelings but also know that this time will pass. This helps children build resilience and reduces anxiety.

Areas of learning:

Developed awareness and concentration

Understanding strategies to help manage feelings

Recognising feelings

Sharing feelings

Communication and language

Literacy

Positive relationships

Building self-esteem

Resources:

- Paper
- Pen

Suitable For: KS1, KS2, SEN

How do you feel?

Place 3 trays at the front of the class with a smiley face, sad face and no facial expression. No facial expression shows the child is not sure how they are feeling on that day. Ask the teaching assistant to observe the children coming into the class. Ask each child to place a counter into the tray to express how they feel that day. This allows teachers to observe how children are feeling and if there are any children needing extra emotional support.

Benefits:

This activity allows the children to express how they feel and makes teachers aware of any child that may need extra emotional support that day. It develops children's expression and gives them the opportunity to gain support if needed. This will help with self-esteem as children build confidence to express themselves and share feelings with others.

Areas of learning:

Recognising feelings

Sharing feelings

Building self-esteem

Resources:

- Sad, happy, no facial expression faces
- Counters
- 3 trays

Suitable For: EY, KS1, KS2, SEN

How can we make ourselves feel better?

Ask the children to write a list of emotions on one side of a piece of paper. Ask them to share their ideas.

Ask the children to put their hand up if they ever feel worried or anxious. This highlights the fact that we all get anxious at times. Discuss with the children what makes them worried or anxious.

Ask them to write down on the other side of the paper how does it make them feel inside their body when they feel anxious. For example, butterflies in the stomach, sweaty palms, heart beating faster, crying. Ask the children to share with the class how they feel.

Ask the children to discuss, and write on the board, what they can do to make themselves feel better when they feel like this. For example, mindful colouring, do something they enjoy, play with their pet, listen to music, go outdoors, play an instrument, focus on something else or practice breathing techniques.

Benefits:

This activity develops children's self-confidence to help themselves when feeling overwhelmed with emotions. It allows children to discover for themselves ways to find comfort when they feel anxious, reducing stress and improving resilience.

Areas of learning:

Understanding strategies to help manage feelings

Recognising feelings

Sharing feelings

Communication and language

Literacy

Positive relationships

Building self-esteem

Resources:

- Paper
- Pen
- Board or IWB

Suitable For: KS1, KS2, SEN

Emotion words

Separate the children into small groups providing each group with an emotion word such as happy, sad, angry, love, peace, calm, grumpy. Ask the children to discuss the words and answer the questions:

- How does this word make you feel?
- What situations make you feel this emotion?

Ask the children to talk about this with the group and share their experience of these emotions writing key points on the board. Explain the importance of children expressing themselves and listening to those around them, supporting one another.

Benefits:

This activity gives children an opportunity to express their feelings and encourage them to share their emotions. It develops their vocabulary and helps them communicate, building self-esteem and improving relationships.

Areas of learning:

Understanding strategies to help manage feelings

Recognising feelings

Sharing feelings

Communication and language

Positive relationships

Building self-esteem

Understanding the world

Resources:

- A range of emotions written on separate paper

- Whiteboard or IWB

Suitable For: KS2, SEN

How does our body feel?

Discuss with the children how our body feels when we are sad/happy/angry/excited/grumpy. Use a spider diagram to share the children's ideas with the class. Use your own examples of how you feel in your body.

Benefits:

This activity gives children an opportunity to express their feelings and encourage them to share their emotions. It develops their vocabulary and helps them communicate, building self-esteem and improving relationships.

Areas of learning:

Developed awareness and concentration

Understanding strategies to help manage feelings

Recognising feelings

Sharing feelings

Communication and language

Positive relationships

Building self-esteem

Understanding the world

Resources:

- Whiteboard or IWB

Suitable For: KS1, KS2, SEN

Colour activity

Using a range of colours ask the children what different colours mean to them. For example, show the children the colour red, ask the children;

- Is this colour a happy/sad/angry colour?
- What emotion does this colour remind you of?
- Why does this colour remind you of this emotion?
- Does this colour remind you of a specific time in your life or a person?

Following this discussion give each child a colour (small coloured piece of paper). Choose specific children in the class or ask each child the following questions;

- What does that colour mean to you?
- What emotion does this colour remind you of?
- Why does it remind you of this emotion?
- If your colour were a sound what sound would it be?

Benefits:

This activity gives children an opportunity to express their feelings through colour. It encourages them to share their emotions and experiences. It develops their vocabulary and helps them communicate, building self-esteem.

Areas of learning:

Developed awareness and concentration

Understanding strategies to help manage feelings

Recognising feelings

Sharing feelings

Communication and language

Recognise what makes them unique

Recognising likes and dislikes

Positive relationships

Building self-esteem

Using imagination

Understanding the world

Resources:

- A range of small pieces of coloured paper

Suitable For: KS1, KS2, SEN

Weather feelings

Provide children with a range of weather symbols for them to choose from to express how they are feeling. This can be used at the start and end of a PSHE session to identify if the session has improved the child's anxiety and stress.

For example, using a sunshine for feeling happy, cloud for feeling okay, dark cloud for feeling grumpy and rain cloud for feeling sad the children can circle the weather symbol to demonstrate how they feel.

Benefits:

This activity allows the children to express how they feel and the teacher to evaluate if a PSHE lesson has been successful. This will help with self-esteem as children build confidence to express themselves and share their feelings with others.

Areas of learning:

Developed awareness and concentration

Recognising feelings

Sharing feelings

Communication and language

Building self-esteem

Resources:

- Weather evaluation
- Pencils

Suitable For: KS2, SEN

Emotions and facial expressions

Ask the children to sit on the carpet facing you. Ask them to show you a grumpy/sad/happy/excited/angry/confused/shocked/laughing face.

Choose children to come to the front and show the class one of these facial expressions. The children on the carpet can guess what type of emotion the child is indicating.

Sit the children in pairs and ask them to face each other. Shout out a range of emotions and ask the children to show this facial expression to their partner.

Provide the children with a mirror and ask the children to look at their reflection, showing a range of emotions.

Benefits:

This fun and interactive emotion activity teaches children a range of emotions and how to identify how another person is feeling. It allows the teacher to recognise how a child is feeling at that moment. This builds self-confidence, relationships, turn taking, patience and self-expression.

Areas of learning:

Developed awareness and concentration

Recognising feelings

Sharing feelings

Communication and language

Physical development

Positive relationships

Building self-esteem

Using imagination

Understanding the world

Resources:

- Mirrors

Suitable For: EY, KS1, SEN

Interactive worry plaque

Interactive worry plaques can be bought online

https://www.artnhobby.ie/fairy-door-interactive-worry-plaque

The aim of the plaque is to allow children to express their worries and then the angels take the worries away. The children press their hand onto the plaque. As the plaque turns red the child tells the plaque their worry. After a couple of seconds the plaque turns green and the worries have been taken away. Explain to the children the importance of expressing any worries and telling a trusted adult.

Benefits:

The plaque is an interactive and fun activity for children to let go of any worries they may be holding on to. It is a visual aid to support anxiety and stress and improve sleep as children let go of their worries.

Areas of learning:

Understanding strategies to help manage feelings

Recognising feelings

Sharing feelings

Communication and language

Using imagination

Resources:

- Interactive worry plaque https://www.artnhobby.ie/fairy-door-interactive-worry-plaque

Suitable For: EY, KS1, KS2, SEN

Emotion puppets

Provide a range of emotion puppets or dolls to create storytelling to help children deal with difficult situations in life.

For example; divorce, a new baby in the family, moving house, moving school. Tell a story with a happy outcome using the puppets or dolls as a prop explaining that any changes in life can be worrying. You can use literature or create your own story.

Include the children, asking them questions about what happened when they were going through this situation, how they felt then and how they feel now.

Each doll or puppet represents a different emotion with diverse facial expressions. The puppets or dolls can be bought from the internet or created during an art lesson.

Benefits:

This activity teaches the children a range of emotions. It provides an opportunity for the teacher to discuss different life situations that the children may find difficult. It develops resilience, confidence, reduces anxiety and reassures the children that although a change can be worrying, once we get used to the new situation we feel better.

Areas of learning:

Recognising feelings

Sharing feelings

Communication and language

Building self-esteem

Understanding the world

Resources:

- Emotion dolls or puppets
- Literature

Suitable For: EY, KS1. SEN

Worry dolls

Discuss with the children about how we feel when we are worried or anxious. Ask the children who they can talk to when they are feeling worried. Explain to them the importance of telling a trusted adult when they are feeling this way.

Give each child a piece of card to create their own personal worry doll. Ask the children to draw around a template of a body, adding a face and clothing and to name the doll. Tell the children to put the doll under their pillow before bed telling it any worries they may have. Choose children to show their worry doll to the class.

Benefits:

Worry dolls are used for children to let go of their worries. This improves sleep and anxiety. It encourages children to express their emotions, developing communication.

Areas of learning:

Understanding strategies to help manage feelings

Recognising feelings

Sharing feelings

Communication and language

Fine motor skills

Using imagination

Developing creativity

Resources:

- Card
- Scissors
- Coloured pencils/pens

Suitable For: KS1, SEN

Pause button

Ask the children to put their right hand on their right side, above the hip. Explain to the children that this is their magic pause button. This button helps us to stop and give our self some time out to feel calm and relaxed. When we feel anxious or frustrated, we can press our pause button and focus on 10 slow, deep breaths in and out through the nose.

Benefits:

This allows children to give themselves some time to stop and relax, to self-regulate and use their breath as a tool to reduce stress.

Areas of learning:

Developed awareness and concentration

Understanding strategies to help manage feelings

Recognising feelings

Sharing feelings

Communication and language

Using imagination

Resources:

No resources

Suitable For: KS1,KS2

SELF-ESTEEM ACTIVITIES

SELF-ESTEEM

Building on a child's self-esteem has a massive impact on their learning. If a child has low self-worth, they believe they cannot learn, so by developing children's confidence through fun and engaging activities, they will be encouraged to believe in themselves and build on resilience.

Paper balls

Ask the children to write down on a piece of paper a question for example:

How many brothers or sisters do you have?

What is your favourite subject in school?

What is your favourite food?

Ask the children to scrunch their paper up and then throw it into the middle of the room. The children will then pick up a paper ball and stand in a circle. Ask them to unravel the ball of paper and answer the question. They can then throw the ball again and choose another ball and answer a different question.

Benefits:

This interactive activity allows the children to get motivated by moving around the room. It builds on communication, confidence and self-esteem as the children answer the questions. This activity is useful for children getting to know each other.

Areas of learning:

Developed awareness and concentration

Sharing feelings

Communication and language

Literacy

Recognise what makes them unique

Recognising likes and dislikes

Physical development

Fine motor skills

Positive relationships

Building self-esteem

Using imagination

Understanding the world

Resources:

- Paper
- Pencils

Suitable For: KS2

Compliment notes

Ask the children to write down some affirmations on paper such as 'You are beautiful', 'You are unique', 'You are kind'. The children will then fold the notes and put them into a small bag. The children can then go around the class and ask their peers to remove a compliment out of the bag.

Benefits:

This activity builds self-esteem communication skills and positive relationships.

Areas of learning:

Communication and language

Positive relationships

Building self-esteem

Developing creativity

Resources:

- Paper
- Pens
- Small bag

Suitable For: KS1, KS2, SEN

Movement

Ask the children to stand on a mat or in a space. Ask the children to close their eyes, listen to the music and move their bodies. This activity can also be completed with their eyes open. Using a range of music, ask the children to express themselves using their bodies. You may want to use music such as calming tunes, classical music, or upbeat dance beats, to allow children to express a range of emotions.

Benefits:

This activity provides children with the space to express their creativity using their body. It allows them to be themselves, be present in the moment and free from judgement, improving their self-acceptance and building self-confidence.

Areas of learning:

Developed awareness and concentration

Physical development

Building self-esteem

Using imagination

Developing creativity

Resources:

- Mat

Suitable For: EY, KS1, KS2, SEN

Pom-pom and cup game

Put the children into pairs. Provide one child with a cup and one with a pom-pom. Ask the children to stand one metre apart. The child with the pom-pom will throw it towards the cup, while the child with the cup tries to catch it. Once the child has caught it three times, they can swap places. Children can also swap places with different peers in the classroom.

Benefits:

This activity is created to promote positive relationships, build self-esteem, eye and hand co-ordination and communication.

Areas of learning:

Developed awareness and concentration

Communication and language

Physical development

Fine motor skills

Positive relationships

Building self-esteem

Resources:

- Pom-poms
- Cups

Suitable For: KS1, KS2, SEN

Copy me game

Ask the children to stand with their hands by their sides and their feet together. Explain to the children that you are the leader, and they will copy your movement. Mindfully and slowly move your hands and feet in different ways, for example, wiggling your fingers, moving the legs up and down or touching the head. The aim is to mindfully and slowly move the body. The children will copy your movements. Then choose specific children to be the leader. Explain that the other children will copy the leader.

Benefits:

This activity is to allow children to be mindful and present in the moment. It promotes focus, awareness, physical development, and concentration. It builds self-esteem and positive relationships.

Areas of learning:

Developed awareness and concentration

Communication and language

Physical development

Fine motor skills

Positive relationships

Building self-esteem

Developing creativity

No resources needed

Suitable For: EY, KS1, KS2, SEN

Scarf swapping

Provide each child with a coloured scarf. Ask the children to walk around the room. When you shout change that means change direction. When you shout swap that means that the children will stop and swap scarves with the person closest to them. The children will then ask the person a question, whilst swapping scarves.

Give the children some examples of questions on the board before the activity begins such as favourite colour, food, football team, best friend, family members etc.

Benefits:

This fun and interactive activity develops communication, self-esteem and motivation. It is a useful activity for children getting to know each other.

Areas of learning:

Developed awareness and concentration

Sharing feelings

Communication and language

Recognise what makes them unique

Recognising likes and dislikes

Physical development

Positive relationships

Building self-esteem

Using imagination

Understanding the world

Resources:

- Board
- Pens
- Scarves

Suitable For: KS1, KS2, SEN

Shout out

Ask the children to lie on the floor and relax the body from the head to the toes, one body part at a time, with their eyes closed. Shout out an affirmation one at a time for the children to repeat after you. Shout the affirmation many times with meaning. You can then say it loud, quiet, slowly:

I am strong

I am brave

I am beautiful

I am courageous

I am amazing

I am loved

I am powerful

I am worthy

You can add other affirmations of your choice.

Ask the children to sit up and write down some affirmations of their own. The children can stand in a circle and take turns shouting their affirmations loudly with meaning encouraging them to feel strong and powerful as they say them.

Benefits:

By helping the children to relax this enables them to quieten their mind and focus on the activity. This activity develops self-esteem, confidence, promotes positivity and can release emotions. It encourages children to recognise all their good qualities.

Areas of learning:

Developed awareness and concentration

Sharing feelings

Communication and language

Recognise what makes them unique

Recognising likes and dislikes

Physical development

Positive relationships

Building self-esteem

Using imagination

Resources:

- Paper
- Pencils

Suitable For: EY, KS1, KS2, SEN

Post it note description game

Choose one child to come to the front of the class and face away from the children. Choose another child to write on a post it note a word such as an animal, object or person of their choice and stick it on the child's back. The child then asks the pupils questions to try and identify what the answer is. The children can only answer questions yes or no.

Benefits:

The child develops communication, vocabulary, self-esteem, patience, turn taking and confidence.

Areas of learning:

Communication and language

Literacy

Positive relationships

Building self-esteem

Using imagination

Understanding the world

Resources:

- Post it notes
- Pencils

Suitable For: KS1, KS2, SEN

Being unique

Put the children into pairs and ask them to discuss how they are different from each other. Give the children some examples such as eye colour, favourite food, family members, and favourite thing to do. The children can write down their differences. When the children have completed the task, ask them to share with the class. Explain that we should not compare ourselves to others as we are all unique and special in our own way.

Benefits:

The children will gain an understanding that we are all different and unique in our own way and should celebrate our differences. This activity builds self-esteem, confidence, communication, vocabulary, and team building.

Areas of learning:

Developed awareness and concentration

Sharing feelings

Communication and language

Recognise what makes them unique

Positive relationships

Building self-esteem

Resources:

- Whiteboard or IWB
- Paper
- Pencils

Suitable For: KS1, KS2, SEN

Similarity game

Ask the children to stand up if they wear glasses, enjoy football, have blue eyes, like the colour green and so on. This activity allows the children to recognise the differences between their peers and celebrate their uniqueness. Choose some children to be the teacher and demonstrate some differences. Explain that if we all looked and behaved the same, with the same voice and personality, life would be uninteresting therefore, we should celebrate our individuality.

Benefits:

This fun and engaging activity helps children recognise both their uniqueness and their similarities to peers, encouraging self-awareness, confidence, and physical development.

Areas of learning:

Developed awareness and concentration

Sharing feelings

Communication and language

Recognise what makes them unique

Positive relationships

Building self-esteem

Resources:

No resources

Suitable For: KS1, KS2 SEN

Compliment activity

Moving from one child to the next around the classroom, ask each child to say something nice about the person next to them. Ask the children to put their hands up and explain how it feels when we give and receive a compliment. Explain to the children that compliments can make people feel better in themselves therefore it is important to share compliments in the classroom.

Benefits:

As some children may not receive many compliments this activity is important for children to understand the power of praise and how it makes them feel receiving and giving compliments to others. Encourage compliments in the classroom. This activity builds self-esteem, confidence, positivity, communication, trust and team building.

Areas of learning:

Developed awareness and concentration

Sharing feelings

Communication and language

Recognise what makes them unique

Positive relationships

Building self-esteem

Resources:

No resources

Suitable For: EY, KS1, KS2, SEN

Speech activity

Discuss with the children the importance of kind words. Ask the children to write down kind and unkind words and discuss how these words make us feel. Ask the children to share their views with the class.

Benefits:

This activity allows the children to express themselves, developing self-esteem, communication, vocabulary, listening skills and relationships.

Areas of learning:

Developed awareness and concentration

Recognising feelings

Sharing feelings

Communication and language

Literacy

Positive relationships

Building self-esteem

Resources:

- Paper
- Pencils

Suitable For: KS1, KS2, SEN

Compliment hat activity

Put the children's names in a hat and ask each child to choose one. Moving from one child to the next ask them to say a compliment to the person they have chosen. Ask the children to put their hands up and explain how it feels when we give and receive a compliment. Explain to the children that compliments can make people feel better in themselves therefore it is important to share compliments in the classroom.

Benefits:

As some children may not receive many compliments this activity is important for children to understand the power of praise and how it makes them feel receiving and giving compliments to others. Encourage compliments in the classroom. This activity builds self-esteem, confidence, positivity, communication, trust and team building.

Areas of learning:

Developed awareness and concentration

Sharing feelings

Communication and language

Recognise what makes them unique

Positive relationships

Building self-esteem

Resources:

- Paper
- Pencil

Suitable For: KS1, KS2, SEN

Vision board

Provide the children with some paper and coloured pencils. Discuss with the children any gaols you might have that you would like to share with the class for example starting a new project, going to a new place, eating different foods and some things you would like to achieve including a positive affirmation.

Ask the children to draw a spider diagram and write down a positive affirmation in the middle. Then either draw pictures or write down some goals they would like to achieve throughout the year around the affirmation.

The children can put this next to their bed and tick off the things they have achieved throughout the year. This allows children to become aware of goal setting and identifying things they would like.

Benefits:

This activity promotes positivity, focus, determination, cognitive development and self-esteem. By the children seeing how far they have come by ticking off things they have achieved, builds on their self-confidence, focus and determination.

Areas of learning:

Developed awareness and concentration

Sharing feelings

Communication and language

Literacy

Mathematics

Recognise what makes them unique

Recognising likes and dislikes

Building self-esteem

Using imagination

Understanding the world

Resources:

- Whiteboard or IWB
- Paper
- Pens/pencils

Suitable For: KS2, SEN

Achievement activity

Ask the children to discuss things they have overcome such as fear when starting school, learning how to do something such as swimming, overcoming a difficult lesson in school. Use the board to write down examples of things you have overcome yourself. Explain to the children that any time we do something new we feel fearful until we get used to it and that fear is a natural emotion.

Benefits:

This activity helps children recognise the importance of resilience. It allows children to become aware that all people feel fearful when we are going through a change. It builds self-confidence, resilience and determination.

Areas of learning:

Developed awareness and concentration

Sharing feelings

Communication and language

Literacy

Recognise what makes them unique

Positive relationships

Building self-esteem

Resources:

- Whiteboard or IWB

Suitable For: KS1, KS2, SEN

Intimidation activity

Discuss with the children ways they may feel intimidated. Ask them to work in pairs to express how it makes you feel when someone intimidates you. The aim of the activity is to get the children to recognise what behaviour is acceptable and allow the children to recognise how another child may feel when they act in a disrespectful or hurtful way. Allow the session to flow.

Benefits:

This activity allows children to express themselves and recognise acceptable behaviour and how our behaviour makes other people feel. This promotes positive behaviour, positive relationships, expression, self-awareness, self-reflection and communication.

Areas of learning:

Developed awareness and concentration

Understanding strategies to help manage feelings

Recognising feelings

Sharing feelings

Communication and language

Positive relationships

Building self-esteem

Understanding the world

Resources:

- Whiteboard or IWB

Suitable For: KS2

Gratitude activity

Discuss gratitude with the children and use examples on the board. Use comparison with other cultures for example education, homes, food to demonstrate how lucky we are. You may want to use pictures as a visual aid to support this activity.

Benefits:

This activity promotes positivity and allows children to develop their geographical knowledge, cognitive development and gratitude.

Areas of learning:

Developed awareness and concentration

Sharing feelings

Communication and language

Understanding the world

Resources:

- Whiteboard and IWB

Suitable For: KS2

Myself activity

Ask the children to write down 3 things they like about themselves. Use examples of what you like about yourself. Choose children to share with the class. Encourage the children to share their ideas to build self- confidence.

Benefits:

This activity develops children's self-confidence, communication and positivity. It encourages children to focus on their good qualities.

Areas of learning:

Developed awareness and concentration

Sharing feelings

Communication and language

Literacy

Recognise what makes them unique

Recognising likes and dislikes

Positive relationships

Building self-esteem

Resources:

- Paper
- Pencils

Suitable For: KS1, KS2, SEN

Staying healthy

Ask the children to write down all the ways to keep themselves healthy and discuss with the class, such as eating healthy foods and giving examples - exercise, meditation, yoga, being mindful, positive relationships and focusing on positivity and gratitude. Ask the children to share their ideas with the class.

Benefits:

This activity allows children to become aware of how to keep themselves healthy, the benefits of this and how it effects our emotions and physical development. It improves self-esteem, physical/emotional development and positivity, encouraging the children to make healthier choices.

Areas of learning:

Developed awareness and concentration

Communication and language

Literacy

Building self-esteem

Understanding the world

Resources:

- Paper
- Pencils

Suitable For: KS1, KS2, SEN

Positivity in school

Ask the children to discuss all the things that are positive about being in school such as making positive relationships, learning new things, having fun, and write down the children's ideas on the board. This allows the children to focus on the benefits of school and positivity.

Benefits:

This activity highlights the importance and positive aspects of going to school. This is particularly beneficial for children who may struggle or have a negative outlook on school. It develops positivity and gratitude.

Areas of learning:

Sharing feelings

Communication and language

Recognising likes and dislikes

Positive relationships

Building self-esteem

Resources:

No resources

Suitable For: KS1, KS2, SEN

Special people activity

Ask the children to discuss all the special people in their life and why they are special. Ask the children to share their findings with the class. Encourage the children to write down as many people as possible and focus on identifying the good qualities in those people and how they support the child in their life. This could include their family members, friends, neighbours, schoolteachers etc.

Benefits:

This activity improves children's relationships, confidence building, positivity, communication and gratitude.

Areas of learning:

Developed awareness and concentration

Recognising feelings

Sharing feelings

Communication and language

Positive relationships

Building self-esteem

Understanding the world

Resources:

- Paper
- Pencils

Suitable For: EY, KS1, KS2, SEN

Unique chart

Ask the children to draw a grid with 6 squares. Ask them to write in each box:

3 positive words to describe yourself

Something you have achieved

A compliment someone has given you

Favourite thing to do

Something you have overcome

If you could travel anywhere in the world where would you go?

Choose children to share with the class. Explain that we should not compare ourselves to others as we are all different but rather celebrate our individuality.

Benefits:

This fun and engaging activity improves children's self-esteem, confidence and communication. It encourages children not to compare themselves to other people and focus on their own individuality.

Areas of learning:

Developed awareness and concentration

Sharing feelings

Communication and language

Literacy

Recognise what makes them unique

Recognising likes and dislikes

Positive relationships

Building self-esteem

Understanding the world

Resources:

- Paper
- Pencils

Suitable For: KS1, KS2, SEN

Body language

Ask the children to stand against a wall in a line. Demonstrate how somebody would walk if they had no confidence with shoulders hunched, eyes facing downwards, back arched, looking sad, walking slowly.

Ask the children how they think you are feeling. Ask them to discuss what body language you were displaying to show you were feeling sad. Ask them to take turns walking towards you looking sad.

Next, demonstrate looking angry by stomping feet, eyes glaring towards them, face looking serious. Again, ask the children how they think you are feeling. Ask them to discuss what body language you were displaying to show you were feeling angry. Ask the children to take turns walking towards you looking angry.

Demonstrate looking confident by looking straight ahead, shoulders back and down, eye contact, smiling, back straight. Again, ask the children how they think you are feeling. Ask them to discuss what body language you were displaying to show you were feeling confident. Ask the children to take turns walking towards you looking confident.

Explain to the children that when you are feeling confident you automatically feel more positive and happier in yourself. Explain that when you are open to other people, they react to you in a more positive way for example by smiling back at you.

Play a game and choose children to demonstrate a feeling through their body language such as sad, happy, confused, excited, frustrated. The other children can guess how that person is feeling.

Benefits:

This activity improves confidence, positivity, positive relationships, self-esteem and communication.

Areas of learning:

Developed awareness and concentration

Sharing feelings

Communication and language

Building self-esteem

Using imagination

Resources:

No resources

Suitable For: EY, KS1, KS2, SEN

Positive opinions activity

Sit the children in a circle or at their table. Ask the children to work in small groups and say 3 good things about each person. This allows children to hear other people's opinions about them in a positive way.

Benefits:

This activity highlights the good qualities in each child building self-confidence, improving relationships and positivity.

Areas of learning:

Recognising feelings

Sharing feelings

Communication and language

Recognise what makes them unique

Positive relationships

Building self-esteem

Resources:

No resources

Suitable For: KS1, KS2, SEN

3 compliments activity

Ask the children to write down 3 compliments someone has given them. Remind the children this can be from a family member, teacher, friend, neighbour. Ask the children to share one of their compliments with the class.

Benefits:

This activity highlights the child's good qualities and reminds them of how other people view them. It builds self-esteem and positivity.

Areas of learning:

Developed awareness and concentration

Recognising feelings

Sharing feelings

Communication and language

Literacy

Recognise what makes them unique

Positive relationships

Building self-esteem

Resources:

- Paper
- Pencils

Suitable For: EY, KS1, KS2, SEN

'My day' activity

At the end of the day ask the children to discuss their favourite part of the day. Give the children some examples such as what has made them smile or laugh, what has inspired them. Ask the children to continue this activity every night at home before going to sleep. This allows the child to focus on positivity and gratitude.

Benefits:

This activity highlights positivity and gratitude. This allows the children to focus on positive aspects of their day rather than negativity.

Areas of learning:

Developed awareness and concentration

Understanding strategies to help manage feelings

Recognising feelings

Sharing feelings

Communication and language

Recognising likes and dislikes

Positive relationships

Building self-esteem

Understanding the world

Resources:

No resources

Suitable For: EY, KS1, KS2, SEN

Journal

Provide each child with a journal or notebook. Ask them to write:

- The date
- How are you feeling today?
- 3 things you are grateful for
- What has been the best part of your day?
- Any other notes

Explain that the children can write in their journal every day to express their emotions and focus on the positive parts of the day.

Benefits:

By promoting positivity and expressing themselves the children can change a negative mindset into a positive one.

Areas of learning:

Developed awareness and concentration

Understanding strategies to help manage feelings

Recognising feelings

Sharing feelings

Communication and language

Literacy

Recognising likes and dislikes

Building self-esteem

Resources:

- Journal or notebooks

Suitable For: KS2, SEN

SECTION TWO - SECONDARY

TEENAGERS KS3/KS4

Teenage years can be challenging as young people are finding out where they belong in the world, developing hormone changes and experiencing peer pressure, along with meeting school targets. The activities in this section focus on emotional well-being and learning ways to look at things from a different perspective, providing life-long tools to reduce stress and anxiety.

MINDFULNESS ACTIVITIES

MINDFULNESS

Mindfulness is when we focus on what is happening in the present moment. Often our mind is on autopilot, focusing on the past or the future. We may be concentrating on something that has hurt us in the past or overthinking something that may not even happen in the future. Both thoughts are a wasted energy as the past has already gone, there is nothing we can do about it, and the future has not yet happened. The more we try to control a situation the more we suffer. We do not know what is going to happen in the future so we must surrender to what is happening right now.

When we consciously focus on what is happening in the moment, we are aware of our senses. For example; if we focus on our listening sense, our mind is concentrating on our listening rather than our monkey mind. When we focus on our sight, we are consciously aware of our surroundings which guides us into the present moment.

The more we practice this, the more aware we become of our negative thoughts and we can bring our mind back to the present again knowing that our thoughts are what create our anxiety.

Mindfulness activities for teenagers help them to focus their mind on their senses reducing their anxiety and stress.

Mindful eating

Give each student a raisin or a piece of popcorn. Ask the students to place the raisin or popcorn in the palm of their hand. In silence ask them to concentrate on looking at their raisin/popcorn. Ask them to think about what colours, shapes, and patterns they can see. Take around one minute to have a good look at their raisin/popcorn.

Ask the students to have a smell of their raisin/popcorn and think about whether it smells sweet/sour/nice/not so nice. Ask the students does their mouth water. Take around one minute to smell the raisin/popcorn.

Ask the students to put the raisin/popcorn into the mouth and move it around with their tongue without biting. Ask them to think about what it feels like. Does it feel hard/soft/smooth/rough/sweet/sour/ does it melt?

Ask the students to bite the raisin/popcorn and listen to the sound. What does it sound like?

Ask individual students to discuss their sensory experience with the rest of the class.

Benefits:

During this focused activity, the students are asked to concentrate on a range of senses. This sensory activity allows students to focus and develop sensory awareness.

Areas of learning:

Developed awareness and concentration

Communication and language

Recognising likes and dislikes

Exploring materials

Fine motor skills

Positive relationships

Building self-esteem

Using imagination

Resources:

- raisin or popcorn

Suitable For: KS3/KS4

Gratitude

Ask the students to draw a spider diagram in groups of four and write down things they are grateful for in their life.

Then ask them to write down things they have been grateful for that week.

Ask them to write down what they are grateful for that day such as someone has smiled at them, opened the door for them, gave them a hug.

Ask the students to share their spider diagram with the class.

Ask the students to write down three things they are grateful each night before they go to sleep.

Benefits:

Gratitude increases happiness by 25%. When we focus our mindset on things we are grateful for rather than negative thoughts this increases our happiness, reducing stress, building resilience, positivity and self-esteem.

Areas of learning:

Developed awareness and concentration

Recognising feelings

Sharing feelings

Communication and language

Literacy

Positive relationships

Building self-esteem

Resources:

- Paper
- Pens

Suitable For: KS3/KS4

Being present

Explain to the students that mindfulness is when we consciously focus on what is happening in that moment using our senses.

For example, if we are thinking about the past, over analysing, over thinking and dwelling on things, this is a waste of energy as it is in the past, it has already gone.

If we are focusing on the future, again this is a waste of energy as we do not know what is going to happen in the future and it is out of our control.

When we are consciously present in the moment, our monkey mind stops over-thinking and worrying because it is the thoughts that create our negative emotions.

Ask the students to sit quietly and focus on their senses, listening, taking in their surroundings, asking what can they feel. Then explain, in that very moment, there is nothing to worry about. It is only the thoughts that come into the mind that create stress and anxiety.

Benefits:

This activity provides the students with a tool to help reduce anxiety and stress. By focusing on the moment this allows them to not over-think, improving their self-awareness and consciousness.

Areas of learning:

Developed awareness and concentration

Understanding strategies to help manage feelings

Recognising feelings

Resources:

No resources

Suitable For: KS3/KS4

Stop and listen

Using a timer, tap a chime or singing bowl ask the students to sit and concentrate on their listening for three minutes. Explain that after three minutes you will ask them what they could hear.

Benefits:

This activity not only allows students to stop and concentrate it also allows them time out of their busy day. By stopping and listening they are focusing their monkey mind away from negative thoughts and anchoring their attention onto their sense of hearing. This is a great activity to practice when feeling anxious or worried. Providing time to connect to themselves and practice self-care. This stimulates their sense of awareness, reducing anxiety and improving cognitive development.

Areas of learning:

Developed awareness and concentration

Communication and language

Literacy

Mathematics

Exploring materials

Fine motor skills

Positive relationships

Building self-esteem

Using imagination

Resources:

- Chime or singing bowl

Suitable For: KS3/KS4

Partner listening

Ask the Students to sit with a partner. Give each partner either the number one or two. Number ones will be the listener, number two's will be the speaker. Explain to the students the speaker has one minute to talk to their partner whilst the listener is not allowed to talk but to consciously listen. After one minute ask the listener what the speaker has said.

Give the students examples of what to talk about such as:

'What makes them feel anxious?'

'What are their favourite childhood memories?'

'What makes them feel happy?'

'Tell your partner something they may not know about you?'

'What's their favourite thing to do?'

You can make your own topic up or ask them to discuss a topic of their choice.

Benefits:

This listening activity stimulates the sense of hearing. This develops students' awareness, self-confidence and listening skills. It allows them time to express themselves and build their self-esteem. It encourages them to speak openly about their feelings and emotions, use their initiative, improving team building skills.

Areas of learning:

Developed awareness and concentration

Understanding strategies to help manage feelings

Recognising feelings

Sharing feelings

Communication and language

Recognise what makes them unique

Positive relationships

Building self-esteem

Understanding the world

Resources:

No resources

Suitable For: KS3/KS4

Count the emotion word listening game

Choose a student to stand at the front of the class and choose an emotion word such as happy, sad, angry, excited, confused, guilty, embarrassed. Using a timer the student will talk for one minute about their chosen emotion, for example; if they have chosen the word happy, they would talk about what makes them feel happy, and how this emotion makes them feel inside.

The other students in the class will use a tally to record how many times the person says the emotion word. After one minute, ask the students how many times they thought they heard the word being said.

Benefits:

This fun, engaging and interactive listening game encourages self-confidence and team building. It develops listening, speech and language skills, awareness, concentration and focus. It provides the students space to express their feelings and understand how different emotions make us feel.

Areas of learning:

Developed awareness and concentration

Sharing feelings

Communication and language

Mathematics

Fine motor skills

Positive relationships

Building self-esteem

Resources:

- Timer

- Paper
- Pen

Suitable For: KS3/KS4

Clap game

Sit the students in a circle. Ask the students to focus on their listening. Start the clapping game by clapping, tapping and clicking in a rhythm of up to 8 movements. For example, clap the hands twice, tap the legs twice, clap, tap, click, click. The student next to them will copy the rhythm and so on around the circle. Choose different students to start the clap.

Areas of learning:

Developed awareness and concentration

Communication and language

Physical development

Positive relationships

Building self-esteem

Using imagination

Developing creativity

Benefits:

This interactive listening game improves concentration, listening skills, awareness, self-confidence, team building, taking turns and memory.

Suitable For: KS3/KS4

Heartbeat stillness

Ask the students to stand up. Using a timer ask them to jump for one minute. After one minute ask them to stand still and place their hand on their heart. Choose some students to explain how their body and heart feels.

Ask the students to take 10 slow deep breaths in and out through the nose. Again, choose students to explain how the heart and body feels now compared to before.

Explain to the students that when we are feeling anxious or worried our hearts beat faster, however, this activity demonstrates the power of slow deep breathing and how it helps the body become much calmer and relaxed.

Benefits:

This activity is a good way for students to gain an understanding of how the breath helps us to feel much calmer and relaxed. By focusing on the breath when our heart is beating fast it enables us to relax ourselves and feel less anxious. When we focus on deep breathing we are quietening the monkey mind. This is due to our negative mindset impacting our emotions and then our bodies. Slow, deep breathing is particularly effective for students who may suffer with panic attacks.

Areas of learning:

Developed awareness and concentration

Understanding strategies to help manage feelings

Recognising feelings

Sharing feelings

Communication and language

Mathematics

Physical development

Positive relationships

Building self-esteem

Resources:

No resources

Suitable For: KS3/KS4

Body language

Ask the students to stand barefoot in a large space. Ask them to close their eyes and take slow deep breaths in and out through the nose, taking their time to focus on different parts of the body. Rolling the shoulders up and down, moving the head slowly from side to side and up and down, moving up and down onto the tiptoes, lifting the toes up and down off and onto the floor, lifting the arms and legs slowly up and down. Ask the students to open their eyes and walk around the room as slowly and mindfully as they can, thinking about each step as they touch the floor with their heel and toes, thinking about the foot lifting off the ground and the other foot lowering.

Areas of learning:

Developed awareness and concentration

Understanding strategies to help manage feelings

Physical development

Fine motor skills

Positive relationships

Benefits:

This physical activity encourages students to slow down and become more mindful of their movement. The activity increases student's physical, spatial and body awareness, reducing anxiety. Grounding activities allow students to connect to the Earth and focus their mind on their sense of touch which reduces stress.

Resources:

No resources

Suitable For: KS3/KS4

Grounding activity

Place a range of materials onto the floor in a line such as artificial grass, water in a tray, pebbles, large sponge and bubble wrap. Ask the students to take turns walking barefoot through each material. The students can be blindfolded. The students then describe what it feels like using their senses, for example; soft, bumpy, smooth, and spikey and then they guess what the material is.

Benefits:

This fun, grounding, sensory activity develops student's balance, body awareness, self-confidence, stimulates their sense of touch and reduces anxiety. Grounding allows students to focus their mind on their senses rather than any negative thoughts.

Areas of learning:

Developed awareness and concentration

Communication and language

Recognising likes and dislikes

Exploring materials

Physical development

Positive relationships

Building self-esteem

Using imagination

Resources:

- A range of materials
- Blindfold

Suitable For: KS3/KS4

Grass grounding

Whilst walking barefoot on some grass, ask the students to create a circle. The students will all face the same way, holding their hands behind their back, as they slowly walk around with their eyes lowered towards the ground. The students will be encouraged to concentrate on their feet touching the ground as they take slow breaths in and out through the nose. Explain to them that this is a relaxation activity as they focus on their heels and toes touching the ground as they walk around.

After the students have slowly and mindfully walked around in a circle several times, ask them to stop. Then explain that this time they will focus on one foot at a time. As they breathe in, the right foot will touch the ground and as they breathe out, the left foot will touch the ground, continue with this rhythm. With each step they will concentrate on their breath, keeping the eyes lowered and hands behind the back.

Benefits:

This grounding, walking meditation allows students to concentrate on their sense of touch. It is a walking meditation as they quieten their mind to focus on the breath and movement collaboratively. This activity improves anxiety, balance, physical development, self-awareness, body-awareness, concentration, and focus. This is a useful activity if students are feeling stressed in the classroom for example before any tests.

Areas of learning:

Developed awareness and concentration

Understanding strategies to help manage feelings

Recognising feelings

Physical development

Building self-esteem

Understanding the world

Resources:

No resources

Suitable For: KS3/KS4

Shell activity

Each student will be given a shell. Ask the students to be silent during this activity until the end when they can share their experience with the class.

The students will place the shell in the palm of the hand. Explain to them that when they first looked at their shell they probably thought it was one colour, but now you want them to mindfully look at their shell and think about whether there is more than one colour that they can see. Can they see more than two colours on their shell? Ask them to observe their shell.

Next, ask the students if they can see any shapes or patterns on their shell, and what is the texture of their shell? Is it rough or smooth? What is the outline shape of their shell? Keep reminding them to have a good look at their shell. Ask them to listen to and smell their shell.

Ask them to turn over the shell and see if it is the same on the other side. What colours, shapes, patterns and textures can they see and feel.

When the students have mindfully observed their shell ask them to share with the class, describing their shell in detail.

Benefits:

This mindful sensory activity allows students to concentrate on their senses, quietening the mind and reducing anxiety.

Areas of learning:

Developed awareness and concentration

Understanding strategies to help manage feelings

Sharing feelings

Communication and language

Recognising likes and dislikes

Exploring materials

Fine motor skills

Positive relationships

Building self-esteem

Understanding the world

Using imagination

Resources:

- Shells

Suitable For: KS3/KS4

Nature walks

Go outdoors with the students for a mindful walk asking them to focus on their surroundings. Discuss with the students about the different sounds they can hear, what they see, smell and touch. Ask them to focus on their slow deep breathing as they take in their environment.

Benefits:

Being outdoors quietens the mind and revitalises the body. Taking deep breaths enables the children to concentrate on the present moment helping develop lung capacity, whilst reducing anxiety and stress.

Areas of learning:

Developed awareness and concentration

Understanding strategies to help manage feelings

Recognising feelings

Communication and language

Physical development

Positive relationships

Building self-esteem

Understanding the world

Using imagination

Resources:

No resources

Suitable For: KS3/KS4

Mindful moment

Give each student a small piece of paper with a time of day such as brushing your teeth, putting your shoes on, walking to school, eating your tea. Ask them to be more aware of their senses each time they are completing the action written on their paper.

For example; when brushing their teeth, ask them to think about the touch of the brush moving around their mouth, the taste of the toothpaste, the toothpaste moving down the throat when they swallow, the bristles touching the gums, the touch of the toothbrush in the hand, the smell of the toothpaste.

This activity is to encourage students to be more aware and mindful in the present moment.

Benefits:

This encourages students to be aware and mindful during their day. When we are more mindful, our mind is focused on the activity at hand and we are living in the present moment. This develops our awareness. The more we practice mindfulness, the more aware we become of our negative thoughts arising and can bring our mind back to the present moment. This activity stimulates the senses, reduces anxiety, and improves cognitive development.

Areas of learning:

Developed awareness and concentration

Understanding strategies to help manage feelings

Fine motor skills

Understanding the world

Resources:

- Paper
- Pens

Suitable For: KS3/KS4

Squiggle

Ask one student to come to the front of the class and draw a squiggle on the board. Ask another student to come and complete the picture using their imagination. The students in the class can then guess what they think the drawing is.

Benefits:

This fun and engaging activity builds self-esteem, team building skills, imagination and creativity, self-confidence.

Areas of learning:

Developed awareness and concentration

Communication and language

Literacy

Fine motor skills

Positive relationships

Building self-esteem

Using imagination

Developing creativity

Resources:

- Board
- Pens

Suitable For: KS3/KS4

Monkey mind activity

Placing the students into groups, provide each group with the word 'monkey mind' written in the middle of a spider diagram. Ask the students to write down their ideas of what a 'monkey mind' may be.

Ask them to discuss their answers with the class.

Explain to the students that we all have a monkey mind which is the voice inside our head. Sometimes our monkey mind can say negative things which then affect our emotions.

Ask them to write down all the negative words they may say to themselves such as 'I can't do this', 'Nobody likes me' or 'I am not good enough'.

Explain that just because our thoughts say negative things it is not always the truth.

Ask them to write down how to change their negative self-talk into a positive one.

For example:

'I can't do this' – 'I can do this'

Benefits:

This activity provides students with an awareness of our negative self-talk. Once they are aware of their negative talk, they can gain an understanding that this is just a thought and not always true. This enables them to think about changing their thought patterns from negative to positive. It increases self-awareness and self-esteem, reducing stress and anxiety.

Areas of learning:

Developed awareness and concentration

Understanding strategies to help manage feelings

Recognising feelings

Sharing feelings

Communication and language

Literacy

Positive relationships

Building self-esteem

Resources:

- Paper
- Pencils
- White board

Suitable For: KS3/KS4

Paper plate mandalas

Provide each student with a paper plate and coloured pencils or pens. Demonstrate on the board what a mandala looks like. Ask the students to create their own mandala using patterns, shapes and colours moving around the plate. You can either start from the outside and work your way in or start from the middle and work your way out.

A mandala is developed through self-expression and creative art therefore it is the students own personal design. Play some calming music to help them feel relaxed.

Benefits:

Mandalas are created through self-expression to express how you feel therefore it is the student's own personal design. By allowing the students time to express themselves through art, they develop their creativity and focus, which reduces stress and anxiety.

Areas of learning:

Developed awareness and concentration

Understanding strategies to help manage feelings

Mathematics

Exploring materials

Fine motor skills

Using imagination

Developing creativity

Resources:

- Paper
- Coloured pencils or pens
- Board or IWB

- Examples of mandalas for students to look at

Suitable For: KS3/KS4

EMOTION ACTIVITIES

EMOTIONS

These emotion activities help teenagers to deal with feelings and look at different ways to deal with difficult situations, helping change a negative mindset into a positive one. They help students to understand how their behaviour affects an outcome and how to take responsibility for their behaviour.

Line of day

Draw a line and explain to the students that this represents your day. The beginning of the line is the beginning of your day and the end of the line is the end of your day.

Draw a smiley face at the beginning of the line explaining that when you woke up you felt happy and content. Move a quarter along the line and draw a picture of a sad face at break-time. Explain that someone had upset you so now you are feeling sad.

Next, explain to the students that this was just one moment in your day and we should not let one small incident affect our whole day.

Continuing along the line, draw a picture of a smiley face at lunchtime, home time and bedtime as you did not let one small incident affect your whole day.

Now ask the students to discuss things that have really affected their day. Discuss how things can upset us at that time and we should allow these feelings to arise, but recognise that it is just a moment in our day, then we let go of the situation rather than dwelling on it.

Explain to the students that strategies can be used such as; meditation, practicing being more conscious in the moment, going for a walk in nature, speaking to people they trust, knowing that any difficult times will pass.

Benefits:

This activity demonstrates how we should not let one incident affect our whole day. This promotes positivity and resilience, reducing stress and anxiety. Using the line as a visual to provide a better understanding of how to deal with negative emotions.

Areas of learning:

Understanding strategies to help manage feelings

Recognising feelings

Sharing feelings

Communication and language

Literacy

Building self-esteem

Understanding the world

Resources:

Interactive whiteboard

Pen

Suitable For: KS3/KS4

Life line

Drawing a line, explain to the students that this represents your life. The beginning of the line is the beginning of life and the end of the line is the end of your life. You may draw a baby at the beginning and an elderly person at the end.

The middle of the line is age 50.

Near the beginning draw a sad face, using an example that parents had gotten divorced and you were feeling sad. Following this incident draw smiley faces until the age of 15 when a grandparent had died then draw another sad face. Continue along the line with happy faces until you document a mix of happy and sad events throughout your life.

The line represents the fact that we all go through difficult times in our life and although we may feel sad for a while, this time will pass.

Ask the students to discuss challenging times in their life and what has helped them get through these times.

Explain the strategies that can be used during these difficult times such as meditation, practicing being more conscious in the moment, going for a walk in nature, speaking to people they trust, yoga, having the kknowledge that any difficult time will pass.

Benefits:

This activity demonstrates how we can use specific strategies to help us when we are going through a challenging time. It demonstrates we have a knowledge that this time will pass, building resilience and coping mechanisms in the process.

Areas of learning:

Understanding strategies to help manage feelings

Recognising feelings

Sharing feelings

Communication and language

Literacy

Building self-esteem

Understanding the world

Resources:

Interactive whiteboard

Pen

Suitable For: KS3/KS4

Art

Ask the students to draw a picture, in silence, using either crayons, coloured pencils or paints. Ask them to express themselves and use their creative skills. Play some calming music to create a relaxing ambience. They can draw whatever they would like.

Then ask the students to think about:

What have they drawn?

Why do they think they have drawn that?

What does this mean?

How does this picture make them feel?

Ask the students if they would like to come up and share their art with the class explaining what they have drawn or painted.

Benefits:

Art is a form of expression and creativity. Allowing the students to express themselves through art is a good way for them to share emotions and ideas if they want to. This activity develops creativity and expression.

Areas of learning:

Developed awareness and concentration

Understanding strategies to help manage feelings

Recognising feelings

Sharing feelings

Communication and language

Recognise what makes them unique

Exploring materials

Fine motor skills

Building self-esteem

Using imagination

Developing creativity

Resources:

- Paper
- Crayons, pencils or paint
- Paint brushes
- Water

Suitable For: KS3/KS4

Stress bucket

Discuss with the students about things that make them stressed or anxious. Using a bucket template demonstrate the things that have made you stressed for example being stuck in traffic.

Provide the students with a template and ask them to write down things that make them anxious and stressed inside the bucket.

Using your bucket template demonstrate to the students that sometimes when our bucket of stress becomes full and overflows, this then affects our daily life, for example; making us feel anxious, having panic attacks or not wanting to socialise.

Draw a tap in your bucket and discuss with the class ways they can help release some of that stress for example practicing meditation, being in nature, telling someone they can trust, doing something they enjoy, mindful colouring, breathing techniques.

Ask the students to go back to their bucket, draw a tap and write down ways they can release some of their stress.

Benefits:

This activity is providing a safe and secure space for students to discuss what situations make them feel anxious. Using the bucket as a visual they can see how once stress fills up it can then become a problem, therefore demonstrating the importance of using strategies to help release some of their stress.

Areas of learning:

Understanding strategies to help manage feelings

Recognising feelings

Sharing feelings

Communication and language

Literacy

Fine motor skills

Positive relationships

Building self-esteem

Resources:

- Bucket template
- pencils

Suitable For: KS3/KS4

Draw emotions

Discuss with the students about different emotions that we might feel. Talk about anger and how this makes us feel inside our body.

Discuss with the students ways we can help ourselves when we feel angry. This could be using a stop button (pausing and taking some deep breaths), breathing techniques, counting to 10, having some time out, going for a walk in nature, practicing meditation or grounding techniques, listening to some calming music or doing some mindful colouring, journaling or art. Encourage the students to come up with their own ideas of how they can help themselves.

Using a body template ask the students to colour code different areas to show how it makes them feel in their body. For example; the student may colour red arms and legs as this part of the body feels hot. The face may be green which is colour coded as feeling tingly and the heart may be colour coded blue for feeling cold. There is no right or wrong way for a student to complete this. It is used for them to express themselves, identify their emotions and may be an opportunity for a student to share their feelings.

Benefits:

This activity is providing a safe and secure space for students to express how they feel. It is providing the student with an opportunity to gain more understanding and awareness of their emotions and how to deal with these emotions once they arise. This will allow them to control their feelings in a more effective way.

Areas of learning:

Developed awareness and concentration

Understanding strategies to help manage feelings

Recognising feelings

Sharing feelings

Communication and language

Literacy

Mathematics

Fine motor skills

Positive relationships

Building self-esteem

Resources:

- Body template
- Coloured pencils or pens

Suitable For: KS3/KS4

Anger – scenario

Discuss with the students and write on the board

- What makes us angry?
- How does it make us feel in the body? (e.g. sweaty palms, clenched teeth, shoulders raised, feeling emotional, tension, lethargic once we calm down)

Ask two students to come to the front of the class. Ask student one to pretend to throw a pencil at student two. Ask student two how they would feel and how they would react.

Ask the students in the class to take one minute to discuss with their partner

- How would you feel if someone threw a pencil at you?
- How would you react?

Discuss with the class their answers and explain that we all feel frustrated at times and that some people are more sensitive than others.

Using the two students again, explain that if the student retaliates with aggression, throws something back, storms out of the class and gets into trouble with the teacher and parents, this behaviour will not make them feel good. Use the examples of how it makes us feel when we are angry to demonstrate the negative impact that anger has on our body and emotions.

Discuss with the class how things could have been different in this case using the examples of things we can do to help ourselves when we feel frustrated. For example; telling someone, deep breathing, time out, counting. Explain that we all have a choice and it is about making the best choice to make us feel good.

Benefits:

Through discussion the students can gain an understanding that we all feel frustrated at times. Providing strategies that students can use to help deal with their emotions will give them the opportunity to help themselves feel calmer in difficult situations. This highlights that we all have choices. This activity develops understanding of emotions, improving resilience, self-awareness, relationships and reduces anxiety.

Resources:

- Whiteboard or IWB

Suitable For: KS3/KS4

The road ahead – choices

Ask the student to fast forward to the age of 25. Ask them to draw a spider diagram, writing their name in the middle. Ask them to write down how they see their life at this age for example having lots of friends, what job would they like, where would they live, where would they go on holiday, what hobbies they would have.

Discuss with the class what they have written.

Ask the students to think about how they will achieve these things, for example; working hard at school, being kind to people, setting goals.

Areas of learning:

Understanding strategies to help manage feelings

Recognising feelings

Sharing feelings

Communication and language

Positive relationships

Benefits:

This activity improves students' focus and determination, creating positivity and developing awareness of how our behaviour and choices create a positive outcome. The students can use their imagination and create specific goals.

Resources:

- Paper
- Pencils

Suitable For: KS3/KS4

Shake the bottle

Explain to the students that you have had a stressful morning. With each stressful occurrence that you discuss, shake the bottle of fizzy drink.

For example; your children would not get ready for school, you could not find your shoes, you were late, your car would not start, you were stuck in traffic.

Explain that the bottle of fizzy drink is representing your frustration.

Now pass the bottle around the students asking them to tell you one thing that may have made them frustrated that day. Once the bottle has moved around the students, ask someone what they think will happen if they opened the bottle.

Explain that this is how we feel sometimes when things keep going wrong and we feel like we are going to explode just like the shaken fizzy drink. Discuss with the students ways to help them during these times, for example; practice some meditation, yoga, calming breathing, stop button, timeout, counting, listen to calming music, be more organised.

Benefits:

The students gain an understanding that we all have difficult and frustrating situations at times. This activity provides them with tools to help deal with negative emotions, improving resilience and reducing anxiety and stress.

Areas of learning:

Developed awareness and concentration

Understanding strategies to help manage feelings

Recognising feelings

Sharing feelings

Communication and language

Positive relationships

Building self-esteem

Resources:

- Bottle of fizzy drink

Suitable For: KS3/KS4

Make a plan

Demonstrate on the board a self-care time management plan creating a chart, with days of the week.

Explain that it is important we have balance in our life and how we need opportunities to include self-care into our day.

Discuss with the students, writing down ideas of things they can do to promote self-care. For example, exercise, reading, nature, doing something they enjoy, meditation, being with friends and family, watching their favourite programme.

Once this is established provide a chart for each student to write down days of the week and the regular things they have to do such as attending school, visiting relatives, completing homework etc. Then include and make time to ensure one self-care activity is included in their day to ensure they are making important self-care time for themselves.

Benefits:

Creating a time management chart allows the students to ensure they include self-care time into their busy day. This is important for building resilience, self-confidence, self-love, self-awareness, organisation skills and reducing stress and anxiety.

Areas of learning:

Developed awareness and concentration

Understanding strategies to help manage feelings

Recognising feelings

Sharing feelings

Communication and language

Literacy

Building self-esteem

Developing creativity

Resources:

- Board
- Pen
- Chart

Suitable For: KS3/KS4

Passing emotions/clouds

Ask the students to create a list of emotions that they may feel. Discuss what situations cause these emotions, encouraging the students to express themselves, their experiences, and feelings.

Explain to the students that emotions are like clouds they come and go. One cloud could represent a sad emotion which passes, one cloud could represent anger which passes.

Ask the students to discuss difficult times they may have been through and how they have got through this period, explaining what emotions they felt. Explain that difficult times pass therefore just like a cloud, emotions come and go.

Benefits:

Students feel overwhelmed when they feel negative emotions, therefore this activity reminds them that it is okay to feel these feelings but also it lets them know that the time will pass. This helps students build resilience and self-esteem, reducing anxiety.

Areas of learning:

Developed awareness and concentration

Understanding strategies to help manage feelings

Recognising feelings

Sharing feelings

Communication and language

Literacy

Positive relationships

Building self-esteem

Resources:

- Paper
- Pen

Suitable For: KS3/KS4

How can we make ourselves feel better?

Ask the students to write a list of emotions on one side of a piece of paper. Ask the students to share their ideas.

Ask the students to put their hand up if they ever feel worried or anxious. This highlights the fact that we all get anxious at times. Discuss with the students what makes them worried or anxious.

Ask them to write down on the other side of the paper how does it make them feel inside their body when they feel anxious. For example, butterflies in their stomach, sweaty palms, heart beating faster, crying. Ask them to share with the class how they feel.

Ask the students to discuss, and write on the board, what they can do to make themselves feel better when they feel like this. For example; mindful colouring, do something they enjoy, play with their pet, listen to music, go outdoors, play an instrument, focus on something else or practice breathing techniques.

Benefits:

This activity develops student's self-confidence, resilience, self-awareness and reduces stress. It allows them to identify ways of helping themselves when feeling different emotions.

Areas of learning:

Understanding strategies to help manage feelings

Recognising feelings

Sharing feelings

Communication and language

Literacy

Positive relationships

Building self-esteem

Resources:

- Paper
- Pen
- Board or IWB

Suitable For: KS3/KS4

Emotion words

Separate the students into small groups providing each group with an emotion word such as happy, sad, angry, love, peace, calm, grumpy. Ask the students to discuss the words and answer the questions:

- How does this word make you feel?
- What situations make you feel this emotion?

Ask the students to talk about this with the class and share their experience of these emotions writing key points on the board. Encourage them to discuss situations where they may have felt that emotion.

Explain the importance of students expressing themselves and listening to those around them, supporting one another.

Benefits:

This activity gives students an opportunity to express their feelings and encourages them to share their emotions. It develops their vocabulary and helps them communicate, building self-esteem and improving relationships.

Areas of learning:

Understanding strategies to help manage feelings

Recognising feelings

Sharing feelings

Communication and language

Positive relationships

Building self-esteem

Understanding the world

Resources:

- A range of emotions written on separate paper
- Board
- Pen

Suitable For: KS3/KS4

How does our body feel?

Discuss with the students how our body feels when we are sad/happy/angry/excited/grumpy. Use a spider diagram to share the student's ideas with the class. Use your own examples of how you feel in your body.

Benefits:

This activity gives students an opportunity to express their feelings and encourage them to share their emotions. It develops their vocabulary and helps them communicate, building self-esteem and improving relationships.

Areas of learning:

Recognising feelings

Sharing feelings

Building self-esteem

Resources:

- Whiteboard or IWB

Suitable For: KS3/KS4

Colour activity

Using a range of colours ask the students what different colours mean to them. For example; show the students the colour red, ask the students

- Is this colour a happy/sad/angry colour?
- What emotion does this colour remind you of?
- Why does this colour remind you of this emotion?
- Does this colour remind you of a time in your life or a person?

Following this discussion give each student a colour (small coloured piece of paper). Choose specific students in the class or ask each student the following questions

- What does that colour mean to you?
- What emotion does this colour remind you of?
- Why does it remind you of this emotion?
- If your colour was a sound what would it be?

Benefits:

This activity gives students an opportunity to express their feelings through colour. It encourages them to share their emotions and experiences. It develops their vocabulary and helps them communicate, building self-esteem.

Areas of learning:

Developed awareness and concentration

Understanding strategies to help manage feelings

Recognising feelings

Sharing feelings

Communication and language

Recognise what makes them unique

Recognising likes and dislikes

Positive relationships

Building self-esteem

Using imagination

Understanding the world

Resources:

- A range of small coloured paper

Suitable For: KS3/KS4

Perception

Discuss with the students about how we can sometimes only see things from our own point of view.

Explain that when someone may be acting awkward or hurtful towards us, this is because they may be going through a difficult time themselves but take it out on us.

For example; someone may be feeling sad through a family break up and is not being their usual self. You may take this personally and think this has something to do with you, however, if we understand that others may be going through a difficult time, we can be more compassionate and not take it so personally.

Benefits:

This group discussion allows students to gain an understanding of compassion for others and how not to take things personally. When we see things from the other person's perspective, we will have more understanding. This then reduces anxiety and develops self-awareness.

Areas of learning:

Developed awareness and concentration

Recognising feelings

Sharing feelings

Communication and language

Building self-esteem

Resources:

No resources

Suitable For: KS3/KS4

Feel the fear

Discuss with the class and write on the board times when the students have felt scared of starting something new. For example, starting a new school, moving to a new house, or learning something new.

Ask them to discuss in groups, writing down how they felt at the time and how they felt once they had overcome the fear and got used to the new situation.

Explain that anything we do that is new can be scary until we get used to the new situation. We all have these nervous feelings but when we continue to overcome them, this is how we grow and try new things.

Benefits:

This activity allows the students to overcome fear and know that change can be positive. Recognising the feelings before and after the change, builds the student's self-confidence and resilience, helping them to challenge themselves.

Areas of learning:

Developed awareness and concentration

Understanding strategies to help manage feelings

Recognising feelings

Sharing feelings

Communication and language

Building self-esteem

Resources:

- Board
- Pen

Suitable For: KS3/KS4

SELF-ESTEEM ACTIVITIES

SELF-ESTEEM

Building on a teenager's self-esteem has a massive impact on their learning. If a young person has low self-worth, they believe they cannot learn, so by developing their confidence through fun and engaging activities, they will be encouraged to believe in themselves and build on resilience.

Paper balls

Ask the students to write down on a piece of paper a question, for example;

How many brothers or sisters do you have?

What is your favourite subject at school?

What is your favourite food?

Ask the students to scrunch their paper up and then throw it into the middle of the room. They will then pick up a paper ball and stand in a circle. Ask them to unravel the ball of paper and answer the question. They can then throw the ball again and choose another ball and answer a different question.

Benefits:

This interactive activity allows the students to get motivated by moving around the room. It builds on communication, confidence and self-esteem as the children answer the questions. This activity is useful for students getting to know each other.

Areas of learning:

Developed awareness and concentration

Sharing feelings

Communication and language

Literacy

Recognise what makes them unique

Recognising likes and dislikes

Physical development

Fine motor skills

Positive relationships

Building self-esteem

Using imagination

Understanding the world

Resources:

- Paper
- Pencils

Suitable For: KS3/KS4

Compliment notes

Ask the students to write down some affirmations on paper, such as 'You are beautiful', 'You are unique', 'You are kind'. The students will then fold the notes and put them into a small bag. The students can then go around the class and ask their peers to remove a compliment out of the bag.

Benefits:

This activity builds self-esteem communication skills and positive relationships.

Areas of learning:

Communication and language

Positive relationships

Building self-esteem

Developing creativity

Resources:

- Paper
- Pens
- Small bag

Suitable For: KS3/KS4

Movement

Ask the students to stand on a mat or in a space. Ask the students to close their eyes, listen to the music and move their bodies. This activity can also be completed with their eyes open. Using a range of music, ask the students to express themselves using their bodies. You may want to use a range of music such as calming tunes, classical music, or upbeat dance beats, to allow students to express a range of emotions.

Benefits:

This activity provides students with the space to express their creativity using the body. It allows them to be themselves, be present in the moment and free from judgement, improving their self-acceptance and building self-confidence.

Areas of learning:

Developed awareness and concentration

Physical development

Building self-esteem

Using imagination

Developing creativity

Resources:

- Mat

Suitable For: KS3/KS4

Pom-pom and cup game

Put the students into pairs. Provide one student with a cup and one with a pom-pom. Ask the students to stand one metre apart. The student with the pom-pom will throw it towards the cup, while the student with the cup tries to catch it. Once the student has caught it three times, they can swap places. Students can also swap places with different peers in the classroom.

Benefits:

This activity is created to promote positive relationships, build self-esteem, eye and hand co-ordination and communication.

Areas of learning:

Developed awareness and concentration

Communication and language

Physical development

Fine motor skills

Positive relationships

Building self-esteem

Resources:

- Pom-poms
- Cup

Suitable For: KS3/KS4

Copy me game

Ask the students to stand with their hands by their sides and their feet together. Explain to the students that you are the leader, and they will copy your movement. Mindfully and slowly move your hands and feet in different ways, for example, wiggling your fingers, moving the legs up and down or touching the head. The aim is to mindfully and slowly move the body. The students will copy your movements. Then choose specific students to be the leader. Explain that the other students will copy the leader.

Benefits:

This activity is to allow students to be mindful and present in the moment. It promotes focus, awareness, physical development, and concentration. It builds self-esteem and positive relationships.

Areas of learning:

Developed awareness and concentration

Communication and language

Physical development

Fine motor skills

Positive relationships

Building self-esteem

Developing creativity

No resources needed

Suitable For: KS3/KS4

Scarf swapping

Provide each student with a coloured scarf. Ask them to walk around the room. When you shout change that means change direction. When you shout swap, that means that the student will stop and swap scarves with the person closest to them. The student will then ask the person a question, whilst swapping scarves.

Give the student some examples of questions on the board before the activity begins such as favourite colour, food, football team, best friend, family members etc.

Benefits:

This fun and interactive activity develops communication, self-esteem and motivation. It is a useful activity for students getting to know each other.

Areas of learning:

Developed awareness and concentration

Sharing feelings

Communication and language

Recognise what makes them unique

Recognising likes and dislikes

Physical development

Positive relationships

Building self-esteem

Using imagination

Understanding the world

Resources:

- Board
- Pens
- Scarves

Suitable For: KS3/KS4

Post-it note description game

Choose one student to come to the front of the class and face away from the other students. Choose another student to write on a post-it note a word such as an animal, object or person of their choice and stick it on the student's back. The student wearing the post-it then asks questions to try and identify what the answer is. The second student can only answer the questions yes or no.

Benefits:

The student develops communication, vocabulary, self-esteem, patience, turn taking and confidence.

Areas of learning:

Communication and language

Literacy

Positive relationships

Building self-esteem

Using imagination

Understanding the world

Resources:

- Post it notes
- Pencils

Suitable For: KS3/KS4

Being unique

Put the students into pairs and ask them to discuss how they are different from each other. Give the students some examples such as eye colour, favourite food, family members, and favourite things to do. The students can write down as many differences as possible. When the student has completed the task, ask them to share with the class. Explain that we should not compare ourselves to others as we are all unique and special in our own way.

Benefits:

The students will gain an understanding that we are all different and unique in our own way and should celebrate our differences. This activity builds self-esteem, confidence, communication, vocabulary, and team building.

Areas of learning:

Developed awareness and concentration

Sharing feelings

Communication and language

Recognise what makes them unique

Positive relationships

Building self-esteem

Resources:

- Whiteboard or IWB
- Paper
- Pencils

Suitable For: KS3/KS4

Stand up comparison game

Ask the students to stand up if they wear glasses, enjoy football, have blue eyes, like the colour green and so on. This fun activity allows the students to recognise the differences and similarities between their peers and celebrate their uniqueness. Choose some students to be the leader and demonstrate some of the differences. Explain that if we all looked and behaved the same, with the same voice and personality, life would be uninteresting therefore, we should celebrate our individuality.

Benefits:

This fun and engaging activity helps students recognise their uniqueness, developing self-awareness, confidence, and physical development.

Areas of learning:

Developed awareness and concentration

Sharing feelings

Communication and language

Recognise what makes them unique

Positive relationships

Building self-esteem

Resources:

No resources

Suitable For: KS3/KS4

Compliment activity

Moving from one child to the next around the classroom ask each student to say something nice about the person next to them. Ask them to put their hands up and explain how it feels when we give and receive a compliment. Explain to the students that compliments can make people feel better in themselves therefore it is important to share compliments in the classroom.

Benefits:

As some students may not receive many compliments, this activity is important for them to understand the power of praise and how it makes them feel receiving and giving compliments to others. Encourage compliments in the classroom. This activity builds self-esteem, confidence, positivity, communication, trust and team building.

Areas of learning:

Developed awareness and concentration

Sharing feelings

Communication and language

Recognise what makes them unique

Positive relationships

Building self-esteem

Resources:

No resources

Suitable For: KS3/KS4

Compliment hat activity

Put the students' names in a hat and ask each student to choose one. Moving from one student to the next ask them to say a compliment to the person they have chosen. Ask the students to put their hands up and explain how it feels when we give and receive a compliment. Explain to the students that compliments can make people feel better in themselves, therefore it is important to share compliments in the classroom.

Benefits:

As some students may not receive many compliments this activity is important for them to understand the power of praise and how it makes them feel receiving and giving compliments to others. Encourage compliments in the classroom. This activity builds self-esteem, confidence, positivity, communication, trust and team building.

Areas of learning:

Developed awareness and concentration

Sharing feelings

Communication and language

Recognise what makes them unique

Positive relationships

Building self-esteem

Resources:

- Paper
- Pencil

Suitable For: KS3/KS4

Achievement activity

In groups ask the students to discuss things they have overcome such as fear when starting school, learning how to do something such as swimming, overcoming a difficult lesson in school and things they have achieved.

Use the board to write down examples of things you have overcome yourself. Explain to the students that any time we do something new we feel fearful until we get used to it and that fear is a natural emotion.

Next, ask the students to write down the things they have overcome and achieved. Ask if anyone would like to share with the class.

Benefits:

This activity helps children recognise the importance of resilience. It allows students to become aware that all people feel fearful when we are going through a change. It reminds them of how strong they are, building on self-confidence, resilience, and determination.

Areas of learning:

Developed awareness and concentration

Sharing feelings

Communication and language

Literacy

Recognise what makes them unique

Positive relationships

Building self-esteem

Resources:

- Board
- Paper
- Pens

Suitable For: KS3/KS4

Intimidation activity

Discuss with the student's ways they may feel intimidated. Ask them to work in pairs to express how it makes you feel when someone intimidates you. The aim of the activity is to get the students to recognise what behaviour is acceptable and allow them to understand how another child may feel when they act in a disrespectful or hurtful way. Allow the session to flow.

Benefits:

This activity allows students to express themselves and recognise acceptable behaviour and how our behaviour makes other people feel. This promotes positive behaviour, positive relationships, expression, self-awareness, self-reflection, and communication.

Areas of learning:

Developed awareness and concentration

Understanding strategies to help manage feelings

Recognising feelings

Sharing feelings

Communication and language

Positive relationships

Building self-esteem

Understanding the world

Resources:

- Board

Suitable For: KS3/KS4

Gratitude activity

Discuss gratitude with the students and use examples on the board. Using technology ask the students to study different cultures and compare them with ours such as education, housing, or food.

Ask the students to discuss their findings.

Benefits:

This activity promotes positivity and allows students to develop their geographical knowledge, cognitive development and gratitude.

Areas of learning:

Developed awareness and concentration

Sharing feelings

Communication and language

Understanding the world

Resources:

- Board
- Pens
- Paper
- Technology

Suitable For: KS3/KS4

Myself activity

Ask the students to write down 10 things they like about themselves or things they have achieved. Use examples of what you like about yourself. Choose students to share with the class. Encourage the students to share their ideas to build self- confidence.

Benefits:

This activity develops student's self-confidence, communication, and positivity. It encourages students to focus on their good qualities.

Areas of learning:

Developed awareness and concentration

Sharing feelings

Communication and language

Literacy

Recognise what makes them unique

Recognising likes and dislikes

Positive relationships

Building self-esteem

Resources:

- Paper
- Pencils

Suitable For: KS3/KS4

Staying healthy

Ask the students to write down all the ways to keep themselves healthy and discuss with the class, such as; eating healthy foods, giving examples - exercise, meditation, yoga, being mindful, positive relationships and focusing on positivity and gratitude. Ask the students to share their ideas with the class.

Benefits:

This activity allows students to become aware of how to keep themselves healthy, the benefits of this and how it affects our emotions and physical development. It improves self-esteem, physical/emotional development and positivity, encouraging the students to make healthier choices.

Areas of learning:

Developed awareness and concentration

Communication and language

Literacy

Building self-esteem

Understanding the world

Resources:

- Paper
- Pencils

Suitable For: KS3/KS4

Special people activity

Ask the students to discuss all the special people in their life and why they are special. Ask them to share their findings with the class. Encourage them to write as many people down as possible and focus on identifying the good qualities in each person and how they support the student in their life.

Benefits:

This activity improves students' relationships, confidence building, positivity, communication, and gratitude.

Areas of learning:

Developed awareness and concentration

Recognising feelings

Sharing feelings

Communication and language

Positive relationships

Building self-esteem

Understanding the world

Resources:

- Paper
- Pencils

Suitable For: KS3/KS4

Unique chart

Ask the students to draw a grid with 6 squares. Ask them to write in each box:

3 positive words to describe yourself

Something you have achieved

A compliment someone has given you

Favourite thing to do

Something you have overcome

If you could travel anywhere in the world where would you go?

Choose students to share with the class. Explain that we should not compare ourselves to others as we are all different but rather celebrate our individuality.

Benefits:

This fun and engaging activity improves students' self-esteem, confidence, and communication. It encourages students not to compare themselves to other people and focus on their own individuality.

Areas of learning:

Developed awareness and concentration

Sharing feelings

Communication and language

Literacy

Recognise what makes them unique

Recognising likes and dislikes

Positive relationships

Building self-esteem

Understanding the world

Resources:

- Paper
- Pencils

Suitable For: KS3/KS4

Body language

Ask the students to stand against a wall in a line. Demonstrate how you would walk if you had no confidence with shoulders hunched, eyes facing downwards, back arched, looking sad, walking slowly.

Ask the students how they think you are feeling. Ask them to discuss what body language you were displaying to show you were feeling sad. Ask them to take turns walking towards you looking sad.

Next, demonstrate looking angry by stomping feet, eyes glaring towards them, face looking serious. Again, ask the students how they think you are feeling. Ask them to discuss what body language you were displaying to show you were feeling angry. Ask them to take turns walking towards you looking angry.

Next, demonstrate looking confident by looking straight ahead, shoulders back and down, eye contact, smiling, back straight. Again, ask the children how they think you are feeling. Ask them to discuss what body language you were displaying to show you were feeling confident. Ask them to take turns walking towards you looking confident.

Explain to the students that when you are feeling confident you automatically feel more positive and happier in yourself. Explain that when you are open to other people, they react to you in a more positive way, for example; by smiling back at you.

Play a game and choose students to demonstrate a feeling through their body language such as sad, happy, confused, excited, frustrated. The other students can guess how that person is feeling.

Benefits:

This activity improves confidence, positivity, positive relationships, self-esteem and communication.

Areas of learning:

Developed awareness and concentration

Sharing feelings

Communication and language

Building self-esteem

Using imagination

Resources:

No resources

Suitable For: KS3/KS4

Positive opinions activity

Sit the students in a circle or at their table. Ask the students to work in small groups and say 3 good things about each person. This allows students to hear other people's opinions about them in a positive way.

Benefits:

This activity highlights the good qualities in each student building self-confidence, improving relationships and positivity.

Areas of learning:

Recognising feelings

Sharing feelings

Communication and language

Recognise what makes them unique

Positive relationships

Building self-esteem

Resources:

No resources

Suitable For: KS3/KS4

3 compliments activity

Ask the students to write down 5 compliments someone has given them. Remind the students this can be from a family member, teacher, friend, neighbour. Ask them to share one of their compliments with the class.

Benefits:

This activity highlights the students' good qualities and reminds them of how other people view them. It builds self-esteem and positivity.

Areas of learning:

Developed awareness and concentration

Recognising feelings

Sharing feelings

Communication and language

Literacy

Recognise what makes them unique

Positive relationships

Building self-esteem

Resources:

- Paper
- Pencils

Suitable For: KS3/KS4

'My day' activity

At the end of the day ask the students to discuss their favourite part of the day. Give the students some examples such as what has made them smile or laugh, what has inspired them. Ask the students to continue this activity every night at home before going to sleep. This allows the student to focus on positivity and gratitude.

Benefits:

This activity highlights positivity and gratitude. This allows the student to focus on positive aspects of their day rather than negativity.

Areas of learning:

Developed awareness and concentration

Understanding strategies to help manage feelings

Recognising feelings

Sharing feelings

Communication and language

Recognising likes and dislikes

Positive relationships

Building self-esteem

Understanding the world

Resources:

No resources

Suitable For: KS3/KS4

Journal

Provide each student with a journal or notebook. Ask them to write:

- The date
- How are you feeling today?
- 3 things you are grateful for
- What has been the best part of your day?
- Any other notes

Explain that the student can write in their journal every day to express their emotions and focus on the positive parts of the day.

Benefits:

By promoting positivity and expressing themselves the students can change a negative mindset into a positive one.

Areas of learning:

Developed awareness and concentration

Understanding strategies to help manage feelings

Recognising feelings

Sharing feelings

Communication and language

Literacy

Recognising likes and dislikes

Building self-esteem

Resources:

- Journal or notebooks

Suitable For: KS3/KS4

SUMMARY

This book has been created as a guide to support children's and young people's social, emotional, and spiritual development through fun and engaging activities. The activities allow them to express their creativity and hold space to communicate how they feel. Many children and young people struggle to show emotion; therefore, these activities are designed to give them the opportunity to express.

It is important to acknowledge how children and young people are feeling as many are suffering with anxiety. Through the practice of mindfulness and meditation they have life-long tools to help deal with emotions and it is the responsibility of the teacher and parents to guide this.

Little Sunshine Mindfulness and Yoga contact details:

If you would like more information on what we offer please contact us:

littlesunshineyoga@outlook.com

www.littlesunshineyoga.co.uk

Twitter: @liverpoolshine

FB: Little Sunshine Mindfulness and Yoga

Linked in: Katie Scott

Printed in Great Britain
by Amazon

67499820R00149